WHEN TWO STREAMS MET

Lessons from India's Freedom Struggle

BHARAT DOGRA, RESHMA BHARTI,
JAGMOHAN SINGH AND MADHU DOGRA

वत्स

Published by
Renu Kaul Verma
Vitasta Publishing Pvt Ltd
2/15, Ansari Road, Daryaganj
New Delhi - 110 002
info@vitastapublishing.com

वत्स an imprint of Vitasta Publishing

ISBN 978-93-86473-93-6

First Edition 2020
MRP ₹299

Editor: Kanagam King
Layout: Labanya Kalita
Cover Design: Somesh Kumar Mishra
Printer: Vikas Computer and Printers, New Delhi

Dedicated to the
Efforts and Struggles for Strengthening
Justice, Equality, Communal Harmony, and
Unity in Diversity in India

This initiative is the result of the combined efforts of four writers to bring out inspiring life-stories of freedom fighters for our times. We hope to continue this effort in future publications.

Effort Coordinator: Bharat Dogra

Contents

Introduction

The freedom movement, extending over two centuries against British rule in India, is one of the most inspiring chapters of Indian history. When we look at the extreme hardships that the freedom fighters were able to face and overcome with smiling determination, we marvel at these people who were able to achieve this and stand up in respect and admiration.

But it is certainly not adequate to merely admire. The same spirit of rising above petty issues to successfully face the biggest challenges of our times in the areas of justice, equality, environment protection, democracy, and peace is certainly needed today. The same determination is needed; similar hard work and preparations are needed. A similar deep commitment to some higher ideals in life is needed.

Despite this clear need, the inspiring stories of even some of our most courageous and committed freedom fighters are fading from public memory. This book is an effort in the direction of remembering those great sacrifices (*zara yaad karo qurbani*) to gather strength and inspiration for facing the very great challenges of the twenty-first century.

Bharat Dogra

BIOGRAPHIES

Bhagat Singh
Lasting Legacy for Justice, Liberty and Equality

Bharat Dogra, Jagmohan Singh, Madhu Dogra

Introduction

Shaheed Bhagat Singh is widely recognised as perhaps the most famous and respected revolutionary of the freedom movement of India. Although he, along with his two comrades Sukhdev and Rajguru, was hanged by the colonial regime at the extremely young age of twenty-three, he had already won so much affection and respect that in vast parts of India his fame rivalled that of Gandhi. This has been acknowledged by the official chronicler of the Congress Party. His death (and that of his two colleagues) was mourned by millions across India, from Punjab (his home province) to Tamil Nadu. Many of them wept openly. Political and other differences were set aside as the vast nation was united by tears over the loss of its most beloved sons. Indeed, there were appeals against this death sentence even from the base of the imperial power, from Britain.

While details of this inspiring saga of Shaheed (Martyr) Bhagat Singh have been published widely, nevertheless there remain significant gaps in acknowledging the many-sided achievements and contributions of this remarkable youth, one of the most accomplished among the young leaders of world history. While his predominant role has been that of a freedom fighter, this encompassed many distinguished roles—as a scholar, writer, journalist, disaster relief worker, civil liberties activist, and socialist ideologue—all of which he performed with great proficiency. Among many dedicated comrades, he emerged as almost a natural leader, a reality acknowledged spontaneously by people. On the lighter side, more by force of circumstances (the need to hide his true identity) he also worked for some time as a school teacher (actually a headmaster) and even a small-time dairy entrepreneur (where he is reputed to have distributed free a substantial portion of the milk to employees and friends, remonstrating with his annoyed mother that milk should be distributed among all).

Even more significant are the gaps relating to acknowledging the contributions which Bhagat Singh and his colleagues also made to the non-violent struggle during the period of their jail-sentences, as also their assertion of the importance of non-violent struggles and sustained organisational work among peasants and workers. Their significant work for resisting violence and discrimination based on religious divide has not received due recognition, as also their commitment to rights of Dalits (castes who faced widespread discrimination as untouchables).

Last but not the least, while Bhagat Singh's many-sided accomplishments at a very young age evoke admiration and awe, the family influences which made this possible have not been adequately explored. Bhagat Singh's remarkable consciousness and yearning for justice even at a young age (twelve to fourteen years) has been frequently cited. We must know what made this possible and contributed to this.

This chapter seeks to fill some of these gaps.

Childhood and Family Influences

Bhagat Singh was born on 28 September 1907 at Banga Village (now in Lyallpur district of Pakistan). At the age of nine he heard about the efforts of the Gadar Party; how 8000 Ghadarites (émigrés) returned from America, Canada, and South East Asia to liberate India. Bhagat Singh was impressed by this, particularly by the nineteen-year-old leader Martyr Kartar Singh Sarabha who became a source of great inspiration. In 1919 many innocent people were killed by security forces in the most cruel way at Jallianwala Bagh, Amritsar. At the age of twelve, Bhagat Singh insisted on going to Amritsar to pay homage to those who were killed and brought back a handful of blood-soaked soil from the site of the massacre. With his sister Amar Kaur he put flowers on this soil, as if paying homage to those who had died. At the age of fourteen, we find him observing closely the massacre at Nankana Sahib, the birth place of Guru Nanak. In November of the same year we find him writing (in a letter to his grandfather) about the preparations of an impending railway strike. At the age of fourteen, we also see him getting involved in the Non-Cooperation Movement and participating in activities like burning of foreign cloth as a protest against colonial exploitation. At the age of fifteen-sixteen, we see him establishing contacts with revolutionaries and immersing himself in studying revolutionary literature. At the age of sixteen, we see him leaving home for some time with a message for his father that his life is now dedicated to the freedom of India.

This is quite an extraordinary childhood and to understand the 'making of Bhagat Singh' we need to understand the equally remarkable family in which Bhagat Singh was born and brought up.

Bhagat Singh's grandfather Arjun Singh was a man of strong feelings for social reforms as well as the freedom of India. He often told stories to his family of his own grandfather Fateh Singh who had helped Muslim tenants to get land rights and later unlike other big landowners, refused an offer to get more land by entering into a deal with the British. This happened at the time of the great struggle for independence in 1857. Refusing the offer, Fateh Singh said that according to the teachings of Guru Gobind Singh, as a principle, we should stand with the struggle for justice.

Arjun Singh carried this tradition further and provided an environment conducive for his three sons to join the freedom struggle and reform movements. He set high standards for maintaining good relationships with farm workers. He provided free health care to the needy and encouraged his wife, Jay Kaur, also to do so. At a time when education of girls was frowned upon, he gave the name 'Vidyawati' to his eldest daughter-in-law (mother of Bhagat Singh). He encouraged his daughters-in-law to carry out various constructive activities to help villagers like educating girls and providing a helping hand to the needy. He, along with his wife and other family members, supported the upbringing of about twenty-two orphan children, most of whom later contributed to the freedom movement with dedication.

At the time of the thread ceremony of his two grandsons Jagat Singh and Bhagat Singh he said, 'I dedicate them to the freedom struggle of the nation.'

The eldest son of Arjun Singh was Kishan Singh (father of Bhagat Singh). At a young age he worked with great dedication for earthquake, flood, and drought relief (Bhagat Singh also later worked with great dedication in flood relief work in Kanpur). Then he joined the freedom struggle with an equally strong resolve, helping in the Gadar Revolutionary Party's efforts, going to jail several times, and enduring much hardship. He was also active in the efforts for improving jail conditions (Again a role that was taken up further by his illustrious son Bhagat Singh).

Kishan Singh's wife Vidyawati supported her husband bravely in his various activities, apart from helping in bringing up many orphan children. At a later stage, her courage and firm resolve received nationwide admiration. When her son Bhagat Singh was hanged and her two other sons Kulbir and Kultar as well as daughter Amar Kaur were arrested, she challenged the colonial government saying, 'You can kill me but you can't bend me.'

No less inspiring for Bhagat Singh was his uncle Ajit Singh. In cooperation with other leading freedom fighters like Sufi Amba Prasad, Lala Har Dayal and Lala Lajpat Rai, he quickly

Sardar Ajit Singh
(Uncle of Bhagat Singh)

took forward many initiatives like farmers' movement against unjust taxes and publication of inspiring literature (Both these aspects were later emphasised by Bhagat Singh also). He led a successful public agitation popularly known as *Pagri Sambhal Jatta*, which forced the colonial rulers to withdraw unjust tax rules imposed on farmers. Ajit Singh impressed the first popular leader of the freedom movement, Lokmanya Tilak, so much that he said that when India becomes free, Ajit Singh should be the first President of India. However due to his brilliance and rapid progress the colonial government was expected to take strong action against Ajit Singh. So at the age of twenty-six he had to leave India and for thirty-seven years he worked for India's freedom from various countries outside India. Bhagat Singh cherished the memories and anecdotes about his uncle.

Ajit Singh's wife Harnam Kaur came from a family with strong Sufi influences. She helped villagers with educational and medical services, and spun a lot of khadi thread (this was an integral part of the various constructive works taken up by the freedom movement).

Arjun Singh's third son (and Bhagat Singh's younger uncle) was named Swaran Singh. He started his social activities by working for orphans and for drought and earthquake relief. Then he participated very actively in the freedom movement including publication of freedom literature. He was arrested and became seriously ill in jail. He was released but couldn't recover and died at the young age of twenty-three. His wife Hukam Kaur continued to help in the family's many struggles.

As a child, Bhagat Singh sympathised with both his aunts. Harnam's husband had to leave the country he loved so deeply. Hukam had lost her husband at a very young age. Thoughtful child that he was, Bhagat linked his family tragedies to the oppressive foreign rule.

Growing up in such a family, Bhagat Singh was constantly exposed to stories of the glaring injustices of foreign rule, the extreme distress of people, and the valour of the people who opposed this injustice. The family had a rich collection of literature on these issues and Bhagat Singh started reading all this at a very young age.

From this family which challenged prevailing social and religious norms and supported reforms, Bhagat Singh got his strong sense of rationality and reasoning based on reality and facts.

This was a family which despite suffering many-sided oppressions and economic loss continued to care for workers, poorer families, and orphans. Bhagat imbibed this strong interest of standing by the poor and deprived people.

This family had tried to embrace what was best in many rich traditions as well as the reform movements and the freedom movement, and all this contributed to the very remarkable qualities seen in Bhagat Singh at a very young age.

Preparing for a Wider and Durable National Role

Bhagat Singh completed the first four years of his education in his village and after that went to Lahore for further studies. Here he heard and read a lot about the valiant struggles of the Gadar Party. About 8000 Indians living abroad had come to India with strong hopes and aspirations of securing the freedom of their country. They did not succeed, but their courage and particularly the leadership role of Kartar Singh Sarabha had a lasting impact on many youths of Punjab (and other parts of India) including Bhagat Singh.

Bhagat Singh's school education was disrupted by his involvement in the freedom movement. Later he had to study hard to re-join the National College at Lahore. Here he came in contact with revolutionaries and read a lot of revolutionary literature. Then to avoid family pressures for marriage, he left for Kanpur at the age of sixteen.

Bhagat Singh's first stay in Kanpur was only for six months but he came here again after some time. His time spent at Kanpur was of course devoted to his revolutionary activities, but it also had some other aspects. Here he was involved in flood-relief work with great dedication. He also worked for some time as a teacher/headmaster in a National School in Aligarh district. He established a close friendship with BK Dutt and learnt Bangla from him to read Kazi Nazrul Islam's works and memoirs of Bengal revolutionaries in their original form.

Above all, in the inspiring company of Ganesh Shankar Vidyarthi, he improved his skills as a journalist and political commentator, and wrote many articles for *Pratap*, the famous newspaper edited by Vidyarthi. His writings continued to progress and were published in several journals. Thus even though several writings of Bhagat Singh have been lost, he has left behind many writings of durable and historical interest which continue to inspire many people specially youth in India even today.

Bhagat Singh accompanied his father Kishan Singh to the Belgaum Congress Session where Kishan Singh introduced him to leaders like Nehru and Subhas, to impress that to play effective role in the freedom struggle one must be highly learned. Here he also had a long sitting with Bengal revolutionary Niralamba Swami.

Back in Punjab Bhagat Singh proved his abilities as an organiser by mobilising people in his village Banga to help activists participating in the liberation of gurdwaras from the control of pro-colonial occupiers. Defying the government's orders to not help any of these activist marchers, Bhagat Singh mobilised rural communities to welcome and provide hospitality to activist marchers passing through their villages.

The success of Bhagat Singh's mobilisation also raised possibilities of his arrest, and so Bhagat Singh went to Delhi. Here, apart from continuing his journalism work, Bhagat Singh also played a very courageous role in the efforts to check communal tensions. His roommate, Deenanath Sidharth Alankar, recalled that Bhagat Singh stepped into very high-risk situations to reason with angry people and calm them down.

A similar prioritisation for resisting communalism and asserting the unity of people is evident in the activities of Naujawan Bharat Sabha. Bhagat Singh teamed up with close comrades like Bhagwati Charan Vohra, Sukhdev, and Ram Chandra to form Naujawan Bharat Sabha, an organisation of youths which motivated them to participate in the wider mobilisation of people for communal harmony, for attaining freedom on socialist basis, and fighting injustice.

Back in Punjab he took keen interest in writing for *Kirti*, an Urdu and Punjabi paper established by Gadrites. He wrote on many topics of concern. His writings about Kakori heroes led to his arrest in 1927.

He was subjected to much harassment and intensive interrogation, but nothing could break him and the authorities had to release him on a bail of Rs 60,000.

The year 1921 saw two world events in contrast, the Indian Non-Cooperation Movement which failed to achieve the desired result and the Irish movement which succeeded in getting dominion status. In 1924 Dan Breen's memoirs named *My Fight for Irish Freedom* was published. Bhagat Singh translated it to Hindi and got it published so that they could understand and learn from the Irish success story.

During his Kanpur days, Bhagat joined the organisation of revolutionaries named Hindustan Republican Association (HRA). However in the Kakori Case several leading members of HRA were arrested. Four of them were sentenced to death. This led to a very difficult situation for the remaining members including Bhagat Singh and the more senior leader Chandra Shekhar Azad. Bhagat Singh went through a period of intense introspection.

As he wrote later,

> 'Up to that period I was only a romantic idealist revolutionary. Up till then we were to follow. Now came the time to shoulder the whole responsibility. Due to the inevitable reaction for some time the very existence of the party seemed impossible. Enthusiastic

comrades—nay, leaders—began to jeer at us. For some time I was afraid that someday I also might not be convinced of the futility of our own programme. That was a turning point in my revolutionary career. "Study" was the cry that reverberated in the corridors of my mind…Study to enable yourself to face the arguments in favour of your cult. I began to study. My previous faith and convictions underwent a remarkable modification. The romance…so prominent amongst our predecessors was replaced by serious ideas. No more mysticism, no more blind faith. Realism became our cult. Use of force justifiable when resorted to as a matter of terrible necessity: non-violence as policy indispensable for all mass movements. So much about methods. The most important thing was the clear conception of the ideal for which we were to fight.'

It was as a result of this intense introspection and discussion based on this, that, when leading members of the HRA from different provinces met for an important review in Delhi (Firoz Shah Kotla) on 8 and 9 September 1928, they took a very important decision to add 'socialist' to the name of their organisation. Thus the new name the organisation took was 'Hindustan Socialist Republican Association' (HSRA). Bhagat Singh played the most important role in this decision. This was to make clear the socialist concept of free India.

Responsibilities of Bhagat Singh also increased as he and Vijay Kumar Sinha were made responsible for the co-ordination of the organisation in various provinces. Bhagat Singh also changed his rustic easily identifiable look by cutting his hair at Ferozepur on the way back from the Delhi meeting.

Events moved at a brisk pace after this. There was a lot of anger in the country at the violence unleashed at the people and leaders who had gathered to protest against the Simon Commission at Lahore. This violence was widely believed to be the cause of Lala Lajpat Rai's death soon after. There was a lot of despondency in the country at the inability to do anything while a national-level leader died from such an attack. The HSRA reckoned that strong action against the perpetrators of this attack would help to turn this inertia into a new confidence to move forward on the path of independence. In a much discussed action in December 1928 a police official Saunders was shot dead (while another police official had to be shot to make the escape possible). Bhagat Singh, Rajguru, and Durga then escaped in clever disguises to Calcutta, where leading revolutionary Bhagwati Charan Vohra received them with warmth and congratulated his wife Durga at the well-planned and daring escape. Here they observed the Congress Session and then moved to BK Dutt's village near Burdwan for further planning. The decision to establish a revolutionary centre at Agra was taken and a library with a good collection of revolutionary books was set up.

The need for further action that could focus people's attention on the limitations and weaknesses of the colonial government's reforms and hence prepare people for a more forward-looking path towards independence was strongly felt by the HSRA. Hence a plan was drawn that when the central legislature would debate highly unpopular bills to curtail civil liberties and curb trade union rights, one or two specially prepared bombs would be thrown in the legislature by HSRA members in such a way that they would cause minimal damage and certainly not any loss of life.

This was precisely what Bhagat Singh and BK Dutt did on 8 April 1929. They threw bombs with such precision and care that apart from a big noise and the resulting mayhem, only a few bruises were caused. Bhagat Singh and Dutt then voluntarily handed their revolvers to security personnel, all the time throwing leaflets explaining their stand and also shouting revolutionary slogans. This was in the spirit of Satyagraha but with a revolutionary zeal, that if you challenge the system then stand with determination to face the consequences and propagate your view and convince the world with your arguments.

Courageous as these actions were, these did not necessarily succeed in the aim of the HSRA to win more widespread support, at least not to the extent that the revolutionaries had hoped for.

But these did influence the politics of the time. The slogans raised in the assembly 'Down with British Imperialism' and 'Long Live Revolution' started echoing everywhere.

More arrests were made than was anticipated and HSRA members were linked to a big conspiracy to overthrow the British imperial rule and in the series of actions the Saunders case was included.

Two-year Battle Fought from Prison
Handcuffed Prisoners Defeat the Biggest Imperial Power

After their imprisonment, despite all limitations and adversities, Bhagat Singh and his comrades, by their courage and noble conduct, were able to inspire and mobilise millions of people for a greater participation in the freedom movement. This period of imprisonment of Bhagat Singh and his close comrades thus became one of the most glorious chapters in the freedom movement of India and indeed in all liberation struggles. During these two years April 1929–March 1931, Bhagat Singh and his close comrades can justly be credited with not only defying but even defeating the world's

Bhagat Singh during his first detention (May 1927 to July 1927) with Gopal Singh Pannu DSP, CID, Lahore (Source: Frontline, 4 January 2019)

biggest imperial power from behind the bars. The more the colonial government tried to repress and torture them, the more reverence and affection they received in the entire country because of the courage and determination with which they faced the onslaught. This is why the colonial power with its vast reach and strength was defeated by its handcuffed prisoners.

Much more than their own defence, Bhagat Singh along with BK Dutt (Batukeshwar Dutt) and other comrades concentrated on focusing attention on rights of all political prisoners and issues concerning this. In the course of the various struggles of the freedom movement, a large number of political leaders (mostly freedom fighters) were all the time being imprisoned and the terrible conditions in jails posed a serious threat to their life and health, much beyond the punishment to which they were sentenced to by the legal system. Bhagat Singh and his close comrades went on fasts ranging from sixty to ninety-five days to demand the essential rights of all political prisoners.

Secondly, despite the fact that the colonial government was violating all norms of justice to speed up the case against Bhagat Singh and his close comrades, denying various essential rights to the accused; Bhagat Singh and his colleagues worked very hard to present their views and ideology in careful, well-thought-out ways. As a result it became increasingly clear to people that these revolutionaries had actually taken all care to save human lives in the Assembly Bombing Case. A terrorist generally tries to take more human lives, whereas these freedom fighters had taken maximum precautions to ensure that there was no loss of human life. This was evident in the way the bombs were prepared, and the way in which these were used. They had also given away their revolvers on their own to the security men, although they could have used these weapons to make good their escape.

It was becoming increasingly clear to the people from the conduct and statements made by the revolutionary prisoners that far from indulging in any indiscriminate violence, they had planned their activities very carefully keeping in view only the interests of their country and the freedom movement for which they were willing to make any sacrifice and bear any hardship.

This became apparent from the courage and nobility with which they faced the torture and beatings. They endured fasting for very long periods. Even as they saw their own health and the health of their dearest friends collapse before their eyes, they did not surrender. Paralysis gradually spread from one part of the body to another part for freedom fighter Jatindra Nath Das, yet he did not break his fast. Prison authorities used to mix milk in the water, to make the revolutionaries break their fast. Instead of drinking this milk-mixed water, the thirsty prisoners simply broke the pitchers containing this water. When the authorities tried to force feed them in a cruel way, the prisoners resisted so much that they were injured. Ultimately fearing loss of life due to force feeding, the jail officials had to discontinue these efforts.

As news of such acts of courage and determination spread, the support for these revolutionaries grew rapidly in the country, just as these young freedom fighters had hoped.

In a paper *Bhagat Singh* as '*Satyagrahi*': *The Limits to Non-violence in Late Colonial India* (Modern Asian Studies 43, 3-2009), Neeti Nair has summarised the impact on the nation:

> 'Soon after news of the hunger strike spread, 30 June (1929) was observed as Bhagat Singh-Dutt Day in a majority of districts in the Punjab. In Lahore, 10,000 people attended a meeting organised by the City Congress Committee... The Tribune reported that thousands of Lahorians had expressed their solidarity with the hunger-striking prisoners by fasting that day...Bhagat Singh and Dutt were hailed as the honour of Punjab and Bengal...Volunteers from the Congress and the youth leagues marched in procession with red banners carrying photographs of the hunger-striking prisoners bearing the inscription "all for country's honour sixteen young men are starving to death".'
>
> 'When the success of these processions unnerved the administration and Section 144 was suddenly imposed, Congress, Ahrar, and Akali leaders including Sardar Mangal Singh and Zafar Ali Khan courted arrest by shouting the newly banned slogan 'Inquilab Zindabad' along with members of the newly banned Naujawan Bharat Sabha.'

> 'The Satyagraha Committee won its first victory when the District Magistrate was forced to modify his order and release the defiant demonstrators. The Naujawan Bharat Sabha celebrated its victory by announcing that 21 July would be celebrated as All India Bhagat Singh-Dutt Day. The proposed programme included fasting, processions, the collection of funds for the Conspiracy Case Defence Committee, and meetings to explain the purpose of the hunger strike and protest the treatment of political prisoners.'
>
> '...Das died on 13 September 1929 after a continuous fast of sixty-three days. On the same day that 50,000 funeral processionists marched through Lahore, the Central Legislative Assembly passed a motion of adjournment to censure the government for their policy regarding the hunger striking prisoners in the Lahore Conspiracy Case...In the Punjab, Drs Muhammad Alam and Gopi Chand Bhargava resigned from the Punjab Legislative Assembly. Subhas Bose led the miles-long funeral procession in Calcutta...Rabindranath Tagore was inspired to compose a song.'
>
> 'Later, when Bhagat Singh, Sukhdev, and Rajguru were sentenced to death, Bhagat Singh Appeal Committees were established in every district of the Punjab. At a Bhagat Singh Day on 17 February 1931, colleges emptied out into streets, 15,000 people met in Lahore. More than 1,38,000 signatures seeking the commutation of the death sentence were sent by the All Punjab Bhagat Singh Appeal Committee to the Viceroy. In Amritsar, a public meeting organised by the Workers and Peasants Party demanded the immediate release of all political prisoners. The Tamil Nadu Congress Committee insisted that commuting the death sentence was an essential condition for peace.'

Indeed the protest against the glaring unjust trial and death sentence even reached Britain where an appeal titled 'Stop the Lahore Executions!' was signed by thousands of people. This appeal stated,

> 'We, the undersigned electors in Great Britain, emphatically protest against your sanction being given to the sentences, including three death penalties, passed by the judge in the

Conspiracy Case at Lahore, India, after a trial, the character of which arouses the gravest misgivings.'

'We are aware that the twenty-seven Indian youths accused in this case were not only tried without a jury but by the special personal instructions of the Viceroy. Extraordinary regulations were adopted to conclude the trial without regard to the usual procedure.'

'We regard the sentences passed under these circumstances as a violation of justice and demand that they should be disallowed by you. If the three death sentences are put into operation, we shall hold you and your Government responsible for sanctioning what amounts to the murder of political opponents under the guise of official judicial sentences.'

'Without entering into the question whether there was any justification at all for the trial of the accused men at Lahore, whose conviction could only be obtained by such extraordinary means, we desire as strongly as possible to press our views upon you that there should be in all cases, without exception, an open, normal trial by a jury of the countrymen of the accused persons.'

Invaluable Contributions for our Troubled Times

It is clear that Bhagat Singh and his colleagues, with hardly any resources and working in very adverse situations, were able to create a massive impact in terms of creating high levels of commitment and courage for the freedom movement. This they achieved by their personal example of great courage and noble conduct, and also by careful planning of how to make the best possible use of their very adverse circumstances to somehow take their message in a very convincing way to people. In all of this Bhagat Singh as strategist played a very significant role. The impact of the fasts and other courageous actions of Bhagat Singh and his colleagues could be specifically seen in the Congress moving rapidly towards the goal of full freedom (Complete Independence) from colonial rule.

He and his colleagues also made it amply clear to people that they did not believe in indiscriminate violence and greatly valued human life. All misunderstandings on this score were cleared by them in their statements.

Bhagat Singh wrote very clearly, 'non-violence as a policy indispensable for all mass movements' while force is justifiable only 'when resorted to as a matter of terrible necessity.' During the trial, Bhagat Singh and BK Dutt said in a joint statement, 'We hold human life sacred beyond words.' When asked to define 'revolution' they said equally clearly that it did not mean the cult of 'bomb and pistol'. A similar message was reiterated at the Punjab Student Conference in Lahore.

Basic changes in the existing system rooted in injustice are needed. The system of capitalism and imperialism has to be confronted on a wider scale to remove the basic causes of exploitation and injustice. Only then conducive conditions will emerge for ending war and establishing real and stable peace based on justice. World-level fraternity based on equality in the true sense was emphasised by Bhagat Singh.

On another aspect of peace, Bhagat Singh gave very high priority to ending all sectarian conflicts based on narrow and aggressive interpretations of religious beliefs. He was very active on this front in Punjab, Delhi, and Kanpur, establishing close collaboration with others like Ganesh Shankar Vidyarthi who were very devoted to this work. The Naujawan Bharat Sabha formed by Bhagat Singh and his colleagues was very active on this front in adverse situations and helped to check the spread of communalism.

Bhagat Singh also gave very high priority to the strong mobilisation of Dalits for ending discrimination and exploitation within Indian society. He assigned great importance to social revolution based on the mobilisation of Dalits and this also was a part of the freedom struggle. He called upon the Dalits to get united and challenge the entire society against the injustices suffered by them for so long. At the same time he warned them against the manipulations of bureaucracy of the capitalist system to misguide and use them for its own ends.

Bhagat Singh called upon the youth to mobilise workers and peasants as they were the real strength of the movement. Bhagat Singh gave equal emphasis to workers and peasants, city slums and village huts.

The establishment of a socialist system was emphasised by Bhagat Singh, as is evident from the fact that largely on his insistence the name of their organisation was changed from 'Hindustan Republican Association' to 'Hindustan Socialist Republican Association'.

All this remains highly relevant for India today and a lot of this is also relevant in the international context. It is amazing that Bhagat Singh as the leading ideologue of his organisation was able to formulate such a mature agenda at the age of twenty to twenty-three years. In spite of being extremely tied up in the various activities of his party or being jailed often, he was able to study and write extensively. Finally, all these ideas could be used in such a way as to inspire millions of people. Bhagat Singh and his comrades faced immense sufferings with great courage and nobility of conduct.

It is the combination of all these achievements that makes Bhagat Singh one of the greatest freedom fighters of India and also one of the most inspiring figures of all liberation struggles who continues to inspire millions of people even today.

* * *

Gandhiji Should Have Launched a Nationwide Movement to Save Bhagat Singh

In the important debate on Gandhiji's efforts to save the lives of Bhagat Singh, Sukhdev, and Rajguru, various points of view have been well articulated.

It should also be pointed out here that the British authorities had sent clear instructions for a hard line against revolutionaries. In this context attention may be drawn to a communication from Secretary of State to Viceroy dated 17 January 1930,

> 'Prime Minister asks me to send you following personal message from himself...Try and avoid action which will force you to deal with masses, but rather pick the responsible leaders and deal with them, whoever and whatever they are. Keep up moral authority of the Government and rally round it those who respect

> law and order, and whose political interests will defend India from revolutionary movements, whilst pursuing evolutionary policy. Maintain policy of reform whilst handling with firm determination revolutionary leaders.'

Some participants in the debate have said that Gandhiji put as much effort as he could under the circumstances, while some have said that he failed to make adequate efforts.

However my view is that the issue of saving the life of Bhagat Singh, Rajguru, and Sukhdev was so important that Gandhiji should have launched a nationwide movement with this demand as the main focus. The most important thing to remember here is that this was possible within the Gandhian framework of non-violence if it is agreed that capital punishment is also a form of violence which needs to be checked. The movement against capital punishment has spoken against death sentence even for the worst criminals. But in the case of Bhagat Singh, Rajguru, and Sukhdev, it was the question of saving the most loved freedom fighters of India.

So, very much within the framework of Gandhian non-violence, a nationwide movement should have been launched demanding that the life of Bhagat Singh, Sukhdev, and Rajguru be saved and capital punishment be abolished in all cases if possible, but at least in the case of all freedom fighters.

Such a movement would have united all sections of the freedom movement and India would have achieved independence within five years or so, and there would have been no partition.

Sri Dev Suman

Poet, Freedom Fighter Who Died Fasting for Eighty-four Days

Madhu and Bharat Dogra

Sri Dev Suman is not widely known today, but he was one of the most endearing and inspiring figures of our freedom movement. He achieved martyrdom after fasting for eighty-four days in Tehri jail at the young age of twenty-nine.

Apart from the main freedom movement in India which was directly ruled by Britain, there were several smaller freedom movements in those kingdoms of India which were supported by British rule. Here also the repression was very cruel. This is evident from the struggles led by Sri Dev Suman in Tehri, a kingdom in the Himalayan region. Sri Dev Suman emerges as a very brave and inspiring representative of these struggles in various kingdoms.

He was also a poet, a writer, and a very endearing young man, known to be extremely soft-spoken and friendly. He was a very considerate and affectionate husband. He had very deep love for his mother and he always sought solace at her feet amidst the extremely difficult life that he had chosen for himself.

Suman was born on 25 May 1915 in Jaul village of Tehri Garhwal district. His father was a dedicated ayurvedic doctor who undertook great risks while visiting seriously ill patients in remote villages. While treating cholera patients he himself contracted the disease and died. Suman was a three-year old child at this time. His mother accepted very bravely the responsibility of bringing up four small children.

Suman was sent to Dehradun for studying. At the very early age of fourteen he was attracted towards the freedom movement led by Mahatma Gandhi. He was imprisoned for two months in jail and beaten with canes for participating in the Salt Satyagraha phase of the freedom movement.

Suman then took admission in Oriental College in Lahore for higher studies, but was expelled soon for his important role in a students' movement.

Suman then moved to Delhi to live with brother Parshuram. Here his talent as a writer and poet flowered and a selection of his poems *Suman Saurabh* was published in 1932. He served in educational, literary, and philanthropic institutions. His growing fame prompted the royals of his home-place Tehri to offer him a job which Suman declined, according preference to avail the opportunity of spending some days in the company of Mahatma Gandhi and Zakir Hussain. In 1936 he played a leading role in the establishment of the Garhwal Seva Sangh, which survives to this day under the name of Himalaya Seva Sangh.

At the age of twenty-three Suman married Vinay Lakshmi. They were a very devoted couple. Both of them were keen that Vinay Lakshmi should continue her education and she soon enrolled at Kankhal College (near Hardwar) where she followed Suman's path in taking up work side-by-side to pay for her educational expenses. She was still studying here when Suman attained martyrdom in Tehri.

Suman soon attracted the attention of national-level leaders like Jawaharlal Nehru at meetings of the Congress Party by his dedicated work as well as exceptional capability to present the main issues of his region. Suman was given a leading role when Praja Mandal for Tehri Kingdom was formed at a meeting in Dehradun in 1939

(This was more or less equivalent to forming the local branch of the Congress Party which led the freedom struggle at the national level).

Thus, at the young age of twenty-four Suman had simply too many responsibilities—rushing at times to Delhi, or Shimla, or Wardha for consultations with senior leaders. Yet he found time to regularly meet villagers of his region. Sunderlal Bahuguna, who later became known worldwide as leader of the Chipko Movement, recalls how at the age of twelve or thirteen he first saw Suman when he had come to meet the villagers there. It was this meeting which inspired the young boy and pushed him towards the freedom movement at a very young age. To this day Sunderlal remembers Suman as the teacher who remained an inspiration source for him throughout his life. Several persons, including senior freedom movement figures like Chandra Singh Garhwali and Paripoornananda Painyuli, have left behind accounts of those days which relate what a deep and inspiring impact this young man had made on them. Despite his growing fame he led an austere life, often preferring to walk long distances to save a little money which he would then donate to Praja Mandal. All this while his dearest wife struggled to meet educational expenses at Kankhal. When his mother once complained in jest that he never gave anything to support her, he replied, 'you have two sons to support you mother, you try to think that you have donated me to those who have no one to support them.' He also found time to do selfless service for patients suffering from serious diseases and also for service in Dalit settlements.

In Tehri, forests rights were being trampled upon and when people gathered to protest against this in Rawai, Diwan Chakradhar Juyal ordered armed men to fire on them, killing many villagers. This tragic episode was known as Jallianwala Bagh of Garhwal. This was followed by a terrible clampdown on all democratic and protest activities, including entirely peaceful ones. Suman continued his work in difficult conditions, and prepared reports on the disturbing conditions in Tehri as well as in Dhami Kingdom (near Shimla), where also people had been fired upon.

In 1940, a conference of migrant Garhwalis was held under the presidentship of Suman in Delhi. He was also elected the convener of the Garhwal sub-division of the Congress Satyagraha Committee. He extended help to striking students of Tehri and travelled to Tehri villages taking the message of prohibition, the charkha, and the freedom movement. For some days he was detained by the police.

Meanwhile, his writings also continued. In particular his writings on repression and freedom movement in the kingdom areas played an important role. Gandhiji was so impressed by his articles on future of Hindi as the national language that he invited him to Wardha.

In 1942, an all-India conference of people's representatives from various kingdoms called upon their rulers to delink themselves from relationships with British governance and to move towards greater accountability towards their people. After returning from this conference, Suman consulted his colleagues and sent a memorandum to the Tehri ruler along similar lines, also asking for ending forced labour (begar) and some unfair taxes. To take this forward, a conference was announced in Tehri but before Suman could reach Tehri for this event he was arrested at Devprayag. He was sent to Dehradun Jail and then to Agra Jail. Several other freedom fighters of the region were also arrested. His jail-mates in Agra later recalled how Suman had won the respect of all other prisoners in a short time. Even in jail, amidst adverse conditions, he continued his study of spirituality, medicine, and freedom movements in kingdoms. By this time he had emerged as one of the most well-informed persons on freedom movements in kingdoms.

He was released after nearly fourteen months of imprisonment and went to Hardwar to meet his wife and the families of several imprisoned freedom-fighters. Then he proceeded to Tehri but was stopped at Chamba and sent to Tehri Jail, just forty-one days after his release from Agra Jail. Tehri Jail had become notorious for its revolting conditions and ill-treatment of political prisoners. There were special instructions to ill-treat and torture Suman to somehow remove him from the freedom struggle.

When Suman refused to sign a letter seeking forgiveness he was caned and very heavy iron chains were put on his feet. Cold water was thrown on his body on very cold nights. He was placed in an isolated cell.

When a completely unfair trial based on false accusations was started, Suman raised demands for a fair trial, lifting restrictions on Praja Mandal, and better treatment of jail inmates. When he did not get any response, he started an indefinite fast on 3 May 1944.

To break his fast he was ill-treated and tortured even more. By this time his disciple Sunderlal Bahuguna had emerged as an activist-journalist. Sunderlal managed to publish news of his ill-treatment so that other parts of the country could know about this. When this news was published Sunderlal was also arrested.

The General Minister of Tehri, Pandit Mauli Chandra tried for his release but when he could not succeed he resigned.

The ill-treatment and torture of Suman continued unabated. As a result he breathed his last on 25 July 1944 after a historic fast of eighty-four days. His dead body was thrown into the Ganga River.

When this news spread, condolence and protest meetings were held in several parts of the country including Delhi, Mumbai, Karachi, Lahore, Varanasi, Hardwar, and Dehradun. Special committees were formed by people's organisations to investigate the circumstances of his death and their reports condemned the ill-treatment, torture, arbitrary arrest, and unfair trial.

The shocking injustice towards a saintly person like Suman leading to his martyrdom at a very young age opened the eyes of the people to the real, highly unjust, and repressive character of the kingdom so that more and more people started opposing it and the freedom movement gathered strength. In his death as in his life Suman strengthened the movement for justice and freedom.

His writings reveal his deep commitment to justice, equality, and social reform. He wrote repeatedly about protecting the rights of women, farmers, and landless Dalits. He was committed to a health system that reached out to remote villages and gave high priority to improved education for all. He was strongly against the spread of alcoholism and regarded this as a great evil. He was committed to strengthening self-reliance of rural communities symbolised by the charkha (spinning-wheel). After independence there was an anti-liquor movement in Badshahi Thaul near Tehri. In this movement the seventy-two-year-old mother of Sri Dev Suman played an important inspirational role despite being ill. In the course of the movement someone asked her about Suman. She pointed towards all the young anti-liquor movement activists standing near her. She said—'they are all my Sumans'.

Jatindra Nath Das
Died for the Rights of Political Prisoners

Bharat Dogra

Jatindra Nath Das breathed his last on 13 September 1929 after a sixty-three-day fast for protecting political prisoners from many-sided injustices. He was only twenty-five years old at that time. He had undertaken this fast together with Shaheed Bhagat Singh and other imprisoned freedom fighters in Lahore Central Jail. In the course of this fast he had to endure great hardships as he was beaten up brutally and efforts to force feed him damaged his lungs. As paralysis started spreading to parts of his body his sufferings increased but still he insisted on continuing his fast. In fact, considering his serious condition, a jail committee had recommended his release but the government did not agree because it feared his great popularity among people.

When he died people gathered in large numbers in Lahore—perhaps over 50,000—as the body was taken towards the railway station. The revolutionary leader Durga Bhabhi had emerged to lead the procession. Wherever the train stopped people were found waiting in thousands to pay their last respects. Some of the biggest gatherings were in Kanpur, led by Ganesh Shankar Vidyarthi and

Jawaharlal Nehru, and in Allahabad, led by Kamala Nehru. At Calcutta when Subhas Chandra Bose came forward at Howrah Railway Station to receive the coffin, the end of the huge procession was just not visible. Some estimates say that over seven lakh people were in the funeral procession in Calcutta.

DR. ALAM AND DR. GOPI CHAND RESIGN.

The Tribune.

VOL. XLIX. NO. 211. LAHORE, SUNDAY, SEPTEMBER 15, 1929. Price : One Anna.

JATINDRANATH DAS PASSES AWAY.

ousands Attend Funeral Procession.

EOPLE SHOWER FLOWERS AND COINS.

Calcutta Corporation Adjourns.

. MOTILAL NEHRU WILL MOVE ADJOURNMENT OF ASSEMBLY

Mr. Jatindranath Das lying dead in Borstal Jail

r. Jatindranath Das passed away at 1-5 p.m. on Friday.

"I am not a Bengali. I am an Indian." Jatin's Parting Words

HARTAL IN LAHORE.

"I AM NOT A BENGALEE"

Calcutta Corporation Adjourns.

Mayor Pays Tribute to Jatin Das.

CONFERENCE AT PT. MOTILAL'S HOUS

Commotion in Simla.

SWARAJISTS AND LADY SCHUSTER'S PARTY

The front page of The Tribune, 15 September 1929. (Reproduced courtesy of the Supreme Court of India Museum. Image taken from www.researchgate.net)

Hence it is clear that Jatindra's fast and death for the rights of political prisoners had made a very deep impact on the people. The hanging of Bhagat Singh, Sukhdev, and Rajguru was still eighteen months away. If Gandhiji had used the time of the martyrdom of Jatindra Das to launch a nationwide movement for protecting rights of political prisoners and at the very least wresting an assurance from the colonial rulers that there would be no capital punishment for any political prisoners, then at this juncture he would have got the maximum response from people and the path for saving the life of Bhagat Singh, Rajguru, and Sukhdev could have been cleared. Alas this was not to be, as the nation missed a golden moment to mobilise people for a highly justified and relevant cause which was very well within the limits of the highly admirable peaceful resistance of Mahatma Gandhi.

It is always tricky to talk about the various ifs of history, but my understanding is that a great mobilisation by Gandhiji would have greatly strengthened the freedom movement at this critical time and at the same time strengthened the socialists and the more courageous elements among the freedom fighters. All this was possible with the overarching Gandhi-led, Congress-led movement. If this had happened, there would have been a great upsurge of socialist and secular elements and communalisation tendencies in India would have been curbed. In these conditions Subhas Bose would not have been compelled to go out and seek an uncertain future.

All this is very relevant in the context of Jatindra Nath Das as here was a young man who was a very committed revolutionary, joining the Anushilan Samiti first and then teaming up with Bhagat Singh and his comrades in the Hindustan Republican Socialist Association, and yet at the age of seventeen he was also an enthusiastic participant in the Non-Cooperation Movement led by Mahatma Gandhi!

In the middle of all this he also found the time to do very well in his studies. The police finally disrupted his BA studies and sent him to Mymensingh Jail. Here he promptly started a fast to improve the conditions of political prisoners. Such was the impact made by the young revolutionary that the Jail Superintendent agreed to express regret and make some amends.

So this young man who lived for only twenty-five years succeeded twice in drawing widespread public attention to the rights of political prisoners and that too in such an effective way that millions of people responded.

Another remarkable aspect of the work of this incredible youth was that his work area included parts of what today are three separate countries—India, Bangladesh and Pakistan. This may be only incidental but nevertheless attention should be drawn to this. There are after all very few people in the world who have been able to do so much work for political prisoners at such a young age, even sacrificing their life for this cause, and then it is all the more compelling to know that memories of this work can be found today in three separate countries.

Hence it will be a fitting tribute to the memory of this courageous freedom fighter and committed human rights activist to observe his death anniversary (13 September) every year as the Day of Justice for Political Prisoners, not just in India, not just in South Asia, but if possible then at world level.

Badshah Khan
Gandhian Struggles in Difficult Conditions

Bharat Dogra and Reshma Bharti

In recent times the spread of religious fanaticism and violence in some parts of Pakistan has been a matter of great concern. This is the land of Pathans (or Pashtuns/Pakhtuns) who generally have been viewed as being prone to violence and revenge.

At the same time it is important to recall that under the inspiring leadership of Khan Abdul Ghaffar Khan (also called Badshah Khan–the King of Khans–and Frontier Gandhi), a highly inspiring and completely non-violent freedom movement had prospered in the same region between 1920–1947, peaking around 1930–1935 with the involvement of nearly a hundred thousand soldiers of peace.

During those days Badshah Khan had successfully raised an 'army' of peaceful 'soldiers' called 'Khudai Khidmatgars' (or servants of God).

Every Khudai Khidmatgar had to take this oath:-

> 'I am a Khudai Khidmatgar; and as God needs no service, but serving his creation is serving him, I promise to serve humanity in the name of God.

> I promise to refrain from violence and from taking revenge. I promise to forgive those who oppress me or treat me with cruelty. I promise to refrain from taking part in feuds and quarrels and from creating enmity. I promise to treat every Pathan as my brother and friend. I promise to refrain from antisocial customs and practices. I promise to live a simple life, to practice virtue and to refrain from evil.
>
> I promise to practice good manners and good behaviour and not to lead a life of idleness. I promise to devote at least two hours a day to social work.'

Describing the importance of this oath for the people of this region, Badshah Khan's biographer, Eknath Easwaran, writes, 'For a Pathan, an oath is not a small matter. He does not enter into a vow easily because once given, a Pathan's word cannot be broken. Even his enemy can count on him to keep his word at the risk of his own life. Non-violence was the heart of the oath and of the organisation. It was directed not only against the violence of British rule but against the pervasive violence of Pathan life.'

During 1930-31 came the real test of endurance of their commitment to non-violence as the colonial police and army rapidly escalated their brutal repression to check the spread of the freedom movement.

According to a report prepared by the Congress Inquiry Committee, a protest demonstration in Qissa Khwani Bazaar was dispersing peacefully when 'all of a sudden two or three armoured cars came at great speed from behind without giving warning of their approach and drove into the crowd. Several people were run over, of whom some were injured and a few killed on the spot. The people were not armed (not even with stones or bricks). The crowd behaved with great restraint, collecting the wounded and dead.'

More people gathered. The troops were ordered to fire. 'Several people were killed and wounded,' the report continues, 'and the crowd was pushed back some distance. At about half past eleven, endeavours were made by one or two outsiders to persuade the crowd to disperse and the authorities to remove the troops and the armoured cars. The crowds were willing to disperse if they were allowed to remove the dead and the injured and if the armoured cars and troops were removed. The authorities, on the other hand, expressed their determination not to remove the armoured cars and troops. The result was that the people did not disperse and were prepared to receive the bullets and lay down their lives. The second firing then began and, off and on, lasted for more than three hours.'

In his study of non-violent movements, Gene Sharp of Harvard includes a description of the firing in Qissa Khwani Bazaar: 'When those in front fell down wounded by the shots, those behind came forward with their breasts bared and exposed themselves to the fire, so much so that some people got as many as twenty-one bullet wounds in their bodies, and all the people stood their ground without getting into a panic. A young Sikh boy came and stood in front of a soldier and asked him to fire at him which the soldier

The Khudai Khidmatgar Activists

unhesitatingly did, killing him. The crowd kept standing at the spot facing the soldiers and were fired at from time to time, until there were heaps of wounded and dying lying about.'

A newspaper of Lahore, which represented the official view, itself wrote to the effect that the people came forward one after another to face the firing and when they fell wounded they were dragged back and others came forward to be shot at. This state of things continued from eleven till five o'clock in the evening.

Such incidents were repeated. The brave Pathans continued to pass the test of endurance and their commitment to peace and non-violence. The result was that within a few months their support increased dramatically. The Khudai Khidmatgars had started with a strength of about one thousand only, but by the end of September there were nearly eighty thousand volunteers.

Another equally inspiring and dramatic development was that the Hindu soldiers of Garhwal Rifles refused to fire on the peaceful Pashtun freedom-fighters, even when they knew that they would get the most severe punishment. In fact these brave soldiers led by Chandra Singh Garhwali told their officers that they could blow them from their guns if they wanted but they would not fire on freedom fighters.

The peaceful resistance spread widely despite the fact that Badshah Khan and other leaders were arrested. His two sons and elder brother were also arrested.

Another inspiring aspect of the movement, very relevant to the present days of the Taliban, is that Pathan women were encouraged to participate actively in the freedom movement and many of them came forward to play an important role. Badshah Khan opposed the purdah system (veil) and emphasised the equality of women.

Murtaza, who had earlier been jailed for murder, also came under the influence of this peaceful freedom movement. Although he could not sustain this non-violence throughout his life, at least for some years he observed it honestly and sincerely. When Badshah Khan's son Ghani interviewed him about this period of his life, he replied, 'I was a little saint for those four years. I tried to live up to my dreams instead of my desires. It was great, it was a miracle. I refused fortunes for a hope and spared lovely girls because they trusted me and looked up to me. You cannot help loving those that love you, and you cannot hurt those that trust you. I tried to live up to what the people thought I was.'

The lessons that one can learn from recalling this glorious phase of non-violent struggles are two. Firstly, the entire Pashtun community should not be given a bad name because of the spread of Taliban in the area. Till as late as 2007–08, they voted for and elected secular political parties. Many of them resisted the spread of Taliban even at the cost of their life. Secondly, this phase of history tells us how the undoubted courage of people who live violent lives full of 'honour' and 'revenge' killings can be harnessed for constructive tasks and struggles for justice.

It is when such efforts are constantly suppressed (Badshah Khan and his followers faced imprisonment and repression even at the hands of Pakistan's government after the expiry of the British rule) that the chances for violent tendencies to be channelized into the path of fundamentalism and religious extremism increase. This is particularly true if the government itself encourages this as it certainly happened in Pakistan for a long time.

Revival of Khudai Khidmatgars in India

Keeping in view the great importance of Khudai Khidmatgars in the entire history of non-violent struggles against injustice as well as service of humanity, the news that this organisation has been recently revived in India, is highly welcome.

Faisal Khan, National Convenor of Khudai Khidmatgars in India says that efforts were being made for quite some time but the formal inaugural meeting took place near the martyrdom site of Mahatma Gandhi in Delhi on 20 January 2011. Following this the membership drive proved to be very successful even in more remote states like Assam and Manipur.

At the follow-up meeting held at the same place on 20 January 2012, several uniformed Khudai Khidmatgars were also present who have special responsibilities for serving in areas which suffer from communal strife and natural disasters. Leading Gandhians expressed their hopes and good wishes for the steady progress of Khudai Khidmatgars in India.

Ganesh Shankar Vidyarthi
Unique Contribution to the Freedom Movement

Bharat Dogra, Reshma Bharti

While several journalists and newspapers made important contributions to the freedom movement, the contribution made by Ganesh Shankar Vidyarthi and his newspaper *Pratap* is unique in some special contexts.

Firstly, this was a rare newspaper which during the critical decade of 1920–31 was as well known for its support of the Gandhi-led Congress movement as it was for its sympathetic coverage of the revolutionary movement led by Shaheed Bhagat Singh and Chandra Shekhar Azad.

Gandhiji and Jawaharlal Nehru had the highest praise for Vidyarthi while Bhagat Singh and his colleagues consulted Vidyarthi on important issues. In addition, Bhagat Singh also worked for *Pratap* for some time as an assistant editor of sorts, also contributing articles under the pen name of Balwant Singh. As a meeting point of these two waves of the freedom movement in a very sensitive period, Vidyarthi and *Pratap* had a unique role unsurpassed by any other editor or newspaper of those days.

Secondly, both as a freedom fighter and a leading editor, Vidyarthi always emphasized the importance of communal harmony and ultimately sacrificed his life at the young age of forty-one for Hindu-Muslim unity while trying to rescue victims of communal violence in 1931.

Thirdly, Vidyarthi and *Pratap* combined their support of the freedom movement with constant coverage of the problems of peasants and workers as well as their struggles. Several detailed reports of the oppression of peasants by zamindars were published. In this context we may mention reports on the peasants of indigo plantations, firing on agitating peasants of Raebareli, and many-sided oppression in Champaran. Other memorable reports published in *Pratap* included reports on the struggles of textile workers and on various forms of slave labour.

To place this in the context of those times, reports which are likely to fetch reporting awards these days invariably fetched prison sentences in those days. Understandably, Vidyarthi had one foot in prison while bringing out *Pratap*. In fact his years of guiding and editing *Pratap* were disrupted with as many as five prison sentences.

In addition, there were other threats all the time including raids on office and press as well as many defamation cases filed by powerful and extremely rich persons and institutions. Perhaps the most difficulties were created by the cases filed in the fiefs of various royals and their *riyasats* (dominion) as even the pretence of a justice system often did not exist here. Undeterred even by this, Vidyarthi went ahead with publishing daring exposes of the oppression faced by people under the rule of royal families like in Bijolia, Gwalior, and Bharatpur.

The prison sentences which Vidyarthi faced time and again strengthened his role as a civil liberties activist and writer. He himself wrote about the terrible conditions of prisons, the tortuous conditions faced by freedom fighters, and the badly needed jail reforms. While himself suffering these problems time and again, this editor with his never-say-die attitude made use of the time available to him in jail to translate several writings of Victor Hugo into Hindi.

Inspiring Life

Starting his life as a journalist in Kanpur with journals like *Saraswati* and *Abhyudaya*, Vidyarthi soon attracted attention due to his hard work and deep commitment to public causes. So when at a very young age of twenty-three he decided to start a weekly magazine called *Pratap*, devoted to his deep social concerns, several friends and supporters like Shiv Narain Mishra and Narayan Prasad Arora came forward to help him. Despite many problems faced by the new magazine and the disruptions created by the government and others, people really needed such a courageous magazine and responded so well that amidst all the other problems a big decision was taken in 1920 to convert this into a daily newspaper.

Subsequently this Kanpur-based newspaper became widely known as the one widely-read media outlet where stories relating to the misdeeds of the colonial government as well the royals in collusion with this regime were most likely to be published and that too in the most fearless way. Although due to jail sentences and legal complications arising from defamation and other cases Vidyarthi had to quit as editor for short intervening periods he came back repeatedly to edit and guide the newspaper started by him. Even during intervening periods when his name may not have appeared as the editor in a formal way, he was widely regarded as the most important pillar of the newspaper.

The growing popularity of the newspaper and its editor and its moving spirit made it increasingly difficult for the colonial government to initiate frequent actions against them without attracting a lot of flak. In 1925–26, Vidyarthi was elected to the UP Legislative Council while in 1929, he was elected to head the Congress in this important province.

The British government was most troubled by this as Vidyarthi had the confidence and support of the Congress as well as the revolutionaries. Vidyarthi was arrested in May 1930 at a time when the popularity of Bhagat Singh and his companions had begun to peak. He came out of prison on 9 March 1931 and immediately plunged deep into important work.

When Bhagat Singh, Rajguru, and Sukhdev were hanged by the colonial government on 23 March, strong protests broke out in various parts of the country; and Kanpur, under the leadership of Vidyarthi, was all set to emerge as a leading centre of such protests. At this stage, to prevent these protests from emerging, communal riots were instigated deliberately and Vidyarthi was killed in these riots while going to the most dangerous places to rescue trapped people.

Gandhi in his tribute said, 'His blood will become the cementing bond for inter-faith harmony.' Jawaharlal echoed, 'In his death he has taught a lesson that we in our life can't equal for years.'

An Editor who Lived and Died for Communal Harmony

If ever an attempt was made to select the most courageous editor of India for all times, it is most likely that the choice will fall on Ganesh Shankar Vidyarthi, an editor who fought British colonial rule for eighteen years at a stretch with one foot in prison and one in his small office. Working on shoestring budgets, he managed right through this period (roughly from 1913 till his death in 1931) to be highly relevant and influential; his newspaper *Pratap* becoming a leading forum for the wider freedom movement as well as various struggles against big feudal and royal forces. Although he was killed at the young age of forty-one, this legendary editor cum freedom fighter cum friend of all exploited people had achieved enough to last several lifetimes.

Although in keeping with the main focus of those times it is his role as a freedom fighter which has been most discussed, this should not lead to a neglect of his other important concerns and efforts. Among these perhaps the most important concern for him was communal harmony. He repeatedly took up this issue in his newspaper and also helped several citizens' efforts in this direction, particularly in Kanpur, the main area of his work. He played a leading role in forming an organization called 'Hindustani Biradari' which organized programs on communal harmony and joint celebrations of various festivals.

Vidyarthi repeatedly warned people against falling prey to communal propaganda. He could foresee that to divert the rising tide of the freedom movement, the forces of imperialism would try to help and incite the narrow communal forces on both sides. So he wrote against this several times. But even he could not have foreseen that his own life would be lost in trying to control this violence.

In the early days of 1931 the popularity of Bhagat Singh and other revolutionaries who had been imprisoned by the British was soaring to the sky. In a different case Vidyarthi was also in jail but he was released just a few days before the hanging of Bhagat Singh, Rajguru, and Sukhdev on 23 March.

These revolutionaries were very close to Vidyarthi and had very high regard for him. In fact it can be said that among all Congress leaders Vidyarthi was probably closest to them. Given his high organization capability and his mass base it was very likely that Vidyarthi would have mobilized perhaps the biggest opposition against the hanging of Bhagat Singh, Rajguru, and Sukhdev. Keeping this in mind, the colonial regime instigated one of the worst communal violences in Kanpur around the same time that the three revolutionaries were executed.

As Vidyarthi had himself just come out of jail, he did not get enough time to mobilize people against this possibility. However once the flames of violence started burning, he made very determined efforts to even single-handedly rescue as many people as he could. Due to the great respect he commanded among Hindus as well as Muslims, he was one person who could venture into the muhallas or colonies of both communities to rescue people. He was seen rescuing people including women of both communities from difficult situations.

It was in the course of these repeated efforts that at some stage he was stabbed and killed. His dead body was recovered much later, after about two days, so the exact time and circumstances of his death remain uncertain, but there are indications that following the death sentence given to Bhagat Singh, Sukhdev, and Rajguru instructions had been given by colonial rulers to eliminate Vidyarthi also, as he was seen as a bridge between the revolutionaries and the Congress, a man who was capable of radicalizing Congress along a more uncompromising path and equally capable of organizing a strong resistance against the hanging of Bhagat Singh, Rajguru, and Sukhdev.

This view was supported in an interview of his daughter Vimla Vidyarthi who has recorded what she and her mother had heard at that time from others. This interview was conducted by Suresh Salil who has edited and compiled the collected works of Ganesh Shankar Vidyarthi. Vimla stated that her father had successfully rescued some Muslim women but then immediately got involved in rescuing some trapped Hindus and at that stage he was attacked and killed. Vimla stated that she saw the killers not as rioters but as persons guided by colonial rulers. She recalled a well-informed aunt stating that weapons were being distributed in several localities and it was being said that the Lion of Kanpur would be killed that day (*Kahat hai ki Kanpur ka sheru mara jai*). Of course the Lion of Kanpur reference was to Vidyarthi. The concluding observation of Vimla was that the killing of Vidyarthi was a part of the same conspiracy which led to the hurried execution of Bhagat Singh, Sukhdev, and Rajguru.

Sufi Amba Prasad
Died Fighting Colonial Powers in Iran

Bharat Dogra

Sufi Amba Prasad was one of our greatest freedom fighters yet he was almost forgotten even on his 100th death anniversary in the year 2017. He is probably remembered more in Iran where he died fighting colonial powers in Shiraz at the age of fifty-eight. Of course most of his life was devoted to the freedom struggle of India. He was also a great journalist and writer.

Sufi Amba Prasad was one of the heroes of the freedom struggle much admired by Shaheed Bhagat Singh. In fact, Sufiji was a frequent visitor to his family home and worked in very close collaboration with Bhagat Singh's uncle—Sardar Ajit Singh. When the going got too difficult for both of them in India and there was apprehension of yet another arrest, they both escaped quietly to Iran where they continued their work in exile.

Amba Prasad was born in Moradabad in 1858. He was born without a hand and when he grew up he used to jokingly tell his friends, 'I must have lost a hand before dying while fighting in the 1857 war of independence. So when I was born again the next year one hand remained missing!'

It is a testimony to the great courage of this revolutionary that despite the missing hand he even engaged in revolver battles with the police, served prison sentences, and of course contributed greatly to the freedom struggle with his writings. It is said about him that he even trained himself to write with his foot.

Having completed his school, college, and law education in Moradabad, Bareilly, and Jalandhar, young Amba Prasad decided to serve his country with his writings in Urdu language in which he excelled from early days. He emerged as a firm promoter of Hindu-Muslim unity. At the age of thirty-two, he started an Urdu weekly.

At the age of thirty-nine he was arrested for his 'seditious' writings. Released in 1899 after serving a two-year prison sentence he immediately plunged into exposing the injustices of the colonial rule. The empire struck back in a more cruel way this time, sentencing him to six years imprisonment and confiscating all his properties. He was subjected to many cruelties in prison. He was denied medicine for his serious illness and the jailor used to taunt him saying, 'Sufi, you still alive?'

Amba Prasad survived all this and on his release contemptuously turned down offers made by colonial rulers to buy his compromise. He joined a bigger newspaper to earn a livelihood but could last there only for a short time because of the constraints placed on his writings.

It was at this stage that he happened to meet Sardar Ajit Singh and they immediately took to each other like long-lost brothers. Their collaboration resulted in rapid strengthening of the anti-colonial work in Punjab and this in turn resulted in increased repression and arrests. Sufiji along with the older brother of Ajit Singh (Sardar Kishan Singh, father of Shaheed Bhagat Singh) escaped to Nepal. However after sometime they were caught and brought back to Lahore. Somehow they avoided a prison sentence. But Sufiji could not remain silent.

He was very active in bringing out literature for the freedom movement and helping the Bharat Mata Book Agency started by Ajit Singh. His new book *The Rebel Messiah* was banned and confiscated.

In 1909, Sufiji started a newspaper *Peshwa* which led to an increased surveillance of his work and activities. When another arrest appeared imminent he escaped to Iran with Ajit Singh to continue the work for the freedom movement while still in exile.

Here, they also got involved with the nationalist activities of Iran. When Ajit Singh had to leave for Turkey, most of the burden of the work in Iran was shouldered by Sufiji at a time when the British were also consolidating their hold over Iran and were on the lookout for Sufi Amba Prasad. True to his calling the never-say-die Sufi had started a newspaper even during his exile in Iran and so it had become easier to trace him.

This ultimately led to a confrontation in Shiraz where Sufiji faced his attackers with a revolver in his (only) left hand. He fought very bravely but was finally overpowered and imprisoned. He was given a death sentence but expired in jail while awaiting the execution of the death sentence. A very large number of Iranians gathered at his funeral.

He had gained very widespread and deep respect in this country. A memorial erected to honour him is still visited by people long after his death.

Courageous Journalist, Uncompromising Editor

The name of Sufi Amba Prasad is remembered with great respect among those editors and journalists who were ever willing to sacrifice anything to serve the cause of the freedom movement in India. In fact he went a step further by starting a newspaper even in Iran to help the oppressed people there when he had to flee to Iran to escape the wrath of the colonial government in India.

There are several aspects of the multifaceted personality of Sufi Amba Prasad which have attracted admiration and respect. He was an accomplished Muslim scholar and such a firm believer in unity of all religions that his closest collaborators were often from other religions. His most important collaborator in preparing literature for the freedom movement was Sardar Ajit Singh. He was a very accomplished Urdu writer and editor and his skills as a reporter and editorial writer on injustice-related issues was a constant thorn in the side of the colonial government.

Amba Prasad's main contribution towards the freedom movement lasted a little over three decades, ending with his death in a prison cell in Iran. During these three decades he brought out at least three newspapers, served three prison sentences, played a leading role in the main publishing house in Punjab which brought out freedom-movement literature and wrote numerous reports and articles against the many-sided injustices of the colonial government. His book on a rebel was confiscated and he was dragged to court for his articles on injustices on charges of sedition.

During his early days his writings were known for their sarcasm. His first Urdu newspaper *Jaamyul Iluk* was started in 1890. His anti-colonial writings led to police action against him and subsequently he was sentenced to an eighteen-month imprisonment in 1897 at the age of thirty-nine.

After his release from prison he started writing a lot against the improper conduct of the representatives of the colonial government in some of the smaller states. This led to another case culminating this time in a six-year imprisonment and confiscation of ancestral property.

After coming out of jail where he was subjected to extreme hardships, Sufi Amba Prasad tried his hand at working for well-established newspapers for some time but it was difficult to work within the various constraints of these newspapers as his main interest was to take the message of the freedom movement to more and more people. He then turned to reporting and writing for *India*, a nationalist newspaper published by Lala Pindi Das where he could write more freely but these writings brought forth again the wrath of the colonial government.

While devoting some time to bringing out books for the movement, Sufi Amba Prasad also decided to bring out a newspaper *Peshwa* from Punjab to better serve the cause of the freedom movement. Unfortunately, however, this newspaper which was started with a lot of difficulty soon lost the guidance of its founder editor as Sufi Amba Prasad along with Sardar Ajit Singh had to escape to Iran to avoid imminent arrest.

In Iran it was quite difficult to settle down in new surroundings but still as the links with local oppressed sections increased Sufi Amba Prasad was keen to write and report about their problems as well. After establishing some local support base particularly among nationalist sections, Amba Prasad was ready to launch a newspaper called *Aab-e-Hayat*.

While the newspaper was well-received, it also helped the British forces which had been looking for Sufi Amba Prasad to get more details regarding his whereabouts. The search ended in a fiercely contested encounter in which Sufi Amba Prasad was overpowered, imprisoned, and sentenced to death.

An effort should be made to bring together and publish writings, at least those that are still available. These writings can be found in the three newspapers edited by him as well as in other newspapers and journals like *India* where he contributed quite a few reports and articles. Similarly several of his books and booklets can be brought together. These are likely to be more accessible in Punjab. His writings can be very useful in understanding several aspects of the impact of colonial rule on people.

Chandra Shekhar Azad
Symbol of Courage for the Freedom Movement

Bharat Dogra

It was the year 1921. The famous Non-Cooperation Movement against colonial rule was making waves in India. At a protest of this movement in Varanasi, a man who had been felled by police lathis was still being beaten in a most cruel way by policemen.

A fifteen-year-old boy who had joined the protest demonstration could not bear to see this cruelty on the fallen helpless man. He picked up a big stone and hit it with force on the head of the policeman who was hitting the man with his baton again and again. The policeman then left the fallen man and rushed after the boy. The boy led them on a merry chase for some time (so that the injured man could be saved) and then disappeared in the narrow lanes of Varanasi.

However the police kept looking for him and managed to nab him later. When the policemen questioned him, he refused to cooperate with them. Then the policemen caned him. These were big canes which could peel the skin.

'Now let us know your real name.'

'Azad' (meaning free).

'The real name, your real name.'

'Azad'

'Okay tell your father's name.'

'Swatantra' (again meaning free)

'Tell real name.'

'Swatantra'

And so this went on. The boy kept repeating Azad and Swatantra. When he was beaten up more, he shouted *Mahatma Gandhi Ki Jai, Bharat Mata Ki Jai*, each time he was beaten.

Even when his body was badly wounded, the young boy did not stop shouting the slogans.

Soon the entire city was talking about his courage and bravery. When he was released from jail, he was carried by people on their shoulders; the entire crowd shouting slogans of the freedom movement.

Within the next few years this young boy emerged as a leader of the revolutionary movement against colonial rule in India. He was very close to other great leaders of this movement including Bhagat Singh and Ram Prasad Bismil.

Chandra Shekhar 'Azad' participated in several daring actions and launched plans for a big movement. Azad had to hide himself at times as a priest, at times as a driver, and in numerous other ways. However despite his very active life as a revolutionary in Jhansi, Kanpur, and other places, the police could not arrest him. He inspired such awe among policemen that at times even when he was standing very close to those searching for him; they could not or did not arrest him. Many in the police and in the administration had a lot of respect for him, but of course they could never reveal this openly.

Azad had an uncanny ability to mix with ordinary people, including *sadhus* (hermits) and often managed to obtain their services for getting several important works of the revolutionary party completed in a very effective way (such as ensuring wide distribution of pamphlets and posters).

In his later days Azad planned some daring jail escapes to secure the release of his jailed comrades including Bhagat Singh but due to some adverse developments these plans could not succeed. He was also thinking of securing help from abroad, particularly Russia.

The police had increased the search for him but he continued to evade them. However, in February 1931, he was probably betrayed by someone and the police force surrounded him in Alfred Park of Allahabad. He fought very bravely with his pistol till he breathed his last.

Chandra Shekhar 'Azad' not only devoted his entire life to the freedom movement of India, but also endured the greatest hardships, and in the process he became a powerful symbol of resisting injustice with courage for all liberation fighters.

Bhagwati Charan Vohra
A Revolutionary Who Deserves Wider Recognition

Bharat Dogra

Bhagwati Charan Vohra was one of the most dedicated revolutionary freedom fighters of India. While some of his close colleagues like Bhagat Singh and Chandra Shekhar Azad became legends in their lifetime and the country has cherished their memory ever since then, somehow Bhagwati Charan Vohra did not become so well known. Of course his name is taken with respect whenever the revolutionary movement is discussed, but still his many-sided contributions deserve wider recognition.

In his early activities we find him playing multiple roles while helping young revolutionaries like Bhagat Singh and Sukhdev in Punjab. As he had relatively better circumstances at that time, having inherited some wealth, his house in Lahore used to be a place where many revolutionaries would meet and were well looked after. He contributed both intellectually and with actions.

His wife Durga was not only a very brave woman but in addition she also shared his passion for sacrificing her all for the freedom movement. Hence both Bhagwati and Durga (together

Bhagwati Charan Vohra with wife Durga and son Shachi

with their small son Shachi) were drawn more and more into the freedom movement.

Bhagwati Charan was known as a selfless person who was willing to take up any hazardous or difficult task for the sake of his party and the freedom movement.

His encouragement was a strong motivating force which led Durga to take up many difficult and daring activities.

Even after several revolutionaries had been arrested, Bhagwati Charan had managed to evade arrest. He was involved in daring plans for arranging the escape of Bhagat Singh and some other revolutionaries from prison. However this plan did not materialize.

One of the hazardous acts in which Bhagwati Charan was involved was the testing of some bombs. It was in the course of this work in Punjab that Bhagwati Charan met with a serious accident and died. Thus this brave freedom fighter died suddenly at a very young age. His death proved to be a major setback for the prison-escape plans of the other freedom fighters. His many contributions to the freedom movement need to be known and recognised at a much wider level.

Birsa Munda
Led the Great Tribal Revolt against the Colonial Rulers

Reshma Bharti and Madhu Dogra

The advent of the British rule led to a great onslaught on land and forest rights of various tribal communities in India. Hence from very early days we find a continuous string of tribal uprisings which resisted the spread of colonial rule with great courage, even though their bows and arrows could not be a match for the much superior weapons and much bigger armies that the rich colonial regime could easily command.

One great and courageous struggle of the Munda tribal community of Chota Nagpur region (Jharkhand) was led and inspired by Birsa Munda, also called Birsa Bhagwan by some of his followers. The struggle of Birsa was a struggle against injustice and oppression but this struggle also included a movement for social reform and for fighting superstitions.

While colonial rule led to disruption of forest and land rights of tribal communities, local moneylenders and landlords who collaborated with colonial rulers also exploited tribal communities very badly. Hence the struggle led by Birsa was also against this exploitation.

Being surrounded by problems on all sides, it was not easy for Birsa to find a way out. He underwent a lot of inner turmoil as he tried to find a way out of the obstacles which appeared to be insurmountable as there was a powerful gang-up of exploiters against the tribal communities, and economic and military might was concentrated in the hands of the exploiters. They also clearly used social and religious contexts in such shrewd ways that these tribal communities who had been so badly exploited also became submissive and their resistance was weakened.

So, Birsa first tried to find ways to strengthen the faith of tribal communities in the many strong qualities of their culture and society, while at the same time getting rid of the superstitions which had weakened them. Birsa also helped to spread modern concepts of hygiene, sanitation, and control of infectious diseases among his people which proved helpful for them.

The next step was to assert land and farming rights, and to oppose the new exploitative practices relating to this. This in turn led to a sort of Non-Cooperation Movement against the various exploiters, local police, and administration. There was strong opposition to *begar* or the practice of forced labour. In 1895 the Mundas made a declaration of self-rule.

This brought forth a big police force for the arrest of Birsa Munda. He was arrested and taken to Ranchi. This in turn led to even more discontent among the tribal communities, while at the same time they increased the social reform and non-cooperation efforts.

When an open trial against Birsa started in Khunti many Mundas participated in the protests bravely and offered themselves for arrest. Fearing increasing protests, the government took the trial back to Ranchi. Birsa was sentenced to two years of rigorous imprisonment.

Instead of being frightened, the Mundas faced the most difficult conditions of famine and oppression with courage and came back in large numbers to welcome Birsa when he was released from prison. Birsa also devoted himself to reorganizing his people for a bigger struggle. Battle preparations were made. Women also participated in a big way in all these efforts.

With a new-found pride in their social identity, the Mundas were getting ready to defend their rights. Some among them who were identified as Birsaits prepared for a more leading role. They also led a high moral life and avoided liquor completely. A program for restoring land and forest rights of the tribals was announced. Birsa's ideas had matured rapidly and he now had a wide vision of social renaissance, community reform, and economic justice. Several tribal sardars or headpersons were gradually integrated to a considerable extent with this movement, but not all of them shared this wide vision of Birsa. Around the years 1898-1899 many villages of Ranchi and Singhbhum districts were in full preparation for a big revolt of liberation. At meetings organised in a democratic spirit Mundas gave their consent for the great struggle. Many revolt leaders left their homes to operate from forests and hills.

The revolt first started with some sporadic attacks which led to bigger confrontations. A big and decisive battle was fought in the Dombari region in 1900. Mundas fought very bravely but their bows and arrows were finally defeated by the firearms of the British army. This defeat was followed by very cruel atrocities against the Mundas to break their resistance. Birsa was also arrested due to the betrayal of some companions. Despite being burdened by heavy chains, Birsa walked with a smiling face towards the jail. Birsa was subjected to the worst torture in jail and he was probably poisoned as well. He died in prison on 9 June 1900.

This struggle made many more people aware of the great injustices that had been inflicted on tribal communities in those times and even the colonial administration had to agree to withdraw several exploitative laws. Birsa and his brave struggles will always occupy a very important place in the freedom struggle.

Ram Prasad Bismil
irth : 11.06.1897 at Shahjahanpur
ging : 19.12.1927 at Gorakhpur jail

Ashfaqullah Khan
Birth : 21.12.1899 at Shahjahanpur
Hanging : 19.12.1927 at Faizabad Jail

Rajendra Nath Lahiri
: 23.06.1901 at Veer Bhoom, Bengal
nging : 17.12.1927 at Gaunda Jail

Roshan Singh
Birth : 22.01.1892 at Shahjahanpur
Hanging : 19.12.1927 at Naini jail, Allahabad

Four Martyrs of Kakori
Messengers of Freedom and Communal Harmony

Bharat Dogra

Stories of the courage and firm determination of the Kakori martyrs have become an integral part of the legends of our freedom movement. The Kakori Case is regarded as an important event in the freedom movement. All four of these martyrs were hanged to death within four days between 17 December and 20 December 1927. These four freedom fighters, known for their great courage and firm resolve, were Ram Prasad Bismil, Ashfaqullah Khan, Rajendra Nath Lahiri, and Roshan Singh.

Ram Prasad and Ashfaqullah have also won widespread acclaim for their poetry. Some of their poems were very widely used in the freedom struggle. Several of these poems have stood the test of time and are still a source of courage and devotion to a great many people.

All the four martyrs conducted themselves with exemplary courage in the midst of great difficulties after their arrest. Their courage and the dignity of their conduct during the imprisonment made a great impact on people and further enhanced the impact of their message of commitment to the freedom movement and communal harmony. They remain a source of inspiration right up to this day and will continue to be so for a very long time.

Ram Prasad Bismil and Ashfaqullah Khan-Epitome of Communal Harmony

Ram Prasad and Ashfaqullah were very good friends, always willing to undergo great hardships to help each other. Several stories of their friendship have passed into folklore. The great friendship of Ashfaqullah Khan and Ram Prasad Bismil has become a symbol of communal harmony. Just before their martyrdom, both of them issued statements calling for Hindu-Muslim unity. In fact Bismil said that his last wish was that Hindu-Muslim unity should be established firmly. Similarly Ashfaqullah appealed to Hindus and Muslims to avoid quarrels and work unitedly for the sake of their country.

The two of them shared some significant similarities. They were both men of extraordinary courage and determination who sacrificed their all at a young age. They both had very large-hearted concerns which went beyond narrow nationalism and they shared the vision of an alternative world based on justice and equality. They and their families had close connections to Shahjahanpur area of Uttar Pradesh (then United Provinces). They shared a common passion for poetry and were good poets themselves.

On the basis of their shared concerns as well as deep affection for each other they became such close friends that their friendship became a legend in their lifetime. It also became a strong symbol and an inspiration for communal harmony.

Ashfaqullah Khan had a natural inclination for rising above any sectarian thinking. His thinking was based on welfare of all people and could not be constrained by any narrow religious identity. Ram Prasad was initially influenced by some narrow views. However study of changes and revolutions in the world soon made him rise above narrow thinking. Hence he soon overcame narrow influences and started thinking in terms of justice and equality at world level.

So initially when Ashfaqullah tried to befriend Ram Prasad, his senior, Prasad was not very enthusiastic. But later realizing the many great qualities of Ashfaqullah and also overcoming his initial prejudice, he embraced Ashfaqullah wholeheartedly. As members of a revolutionary group, they participated together in many dangerous exploits and assignments. The leadership role was more with Ram Prasad, but Ashfaqullah played a very courageous role and Ram Prasad realised as a leader that Ashfaqullah was one colleague who could always be trusted.

Ram Prasad has written that he soon started regarding Ashfaqullah as his younger brother. This pleased Ashfaqullah, but he also yearned to be an equal colleague. This desire too was soon fulfilled as the two started going together on risky ventures as members of a revolutionary party.

There is a popular story about their close friendship. Once Ashfaqullah fell seriously ill and in his delirium he repeatedly called out 'Ram' 'Ram'. Some of the elder members of his family felt that he had fallen too much under the influence of the Hindu religion and were upset. A friend then arrived and cleared the mystery. Then Ram Prasad was called and when he sat by the side of Ashfaqullah and talked to him most affectionately, family members understood that Ashfaqullah was calling out only for this Ram. This timely arrival also helped in the recovery of Ashfaqullah.

Some of Ram Prasad's Hindu colleagues were upset that he was placing too great a trust in a 'Muslim', but in his leadership role Ram Prasad never wavered in his deep trust of Ashfaqullah and Ashfaqullah fully honoured this trust placed in him. Till his last moments, Ashfaqullah continued to be a devout Muslim and tried his best to bring in more members of his community to the path of the freedom movement.

Ashfaqullah popularised Hindi in his own community, but at the same time asked Ram Prasad to also write in Urdu so that his community members could also read his revolutionary writings.

When death sentence was announced for both of them (and two others Rajendra Lahri and Thakur Roshan Singh) in the Kakori Case, it was widely seen as most unjust as there were no grounds for a death sentence. It was only a dacoity case but one stray fire had resulted in the accidental death of a person. It was not known

Kakori Heroes:
photographed at Lucknow Jail in prisoners' uniforms on 6.4.1927

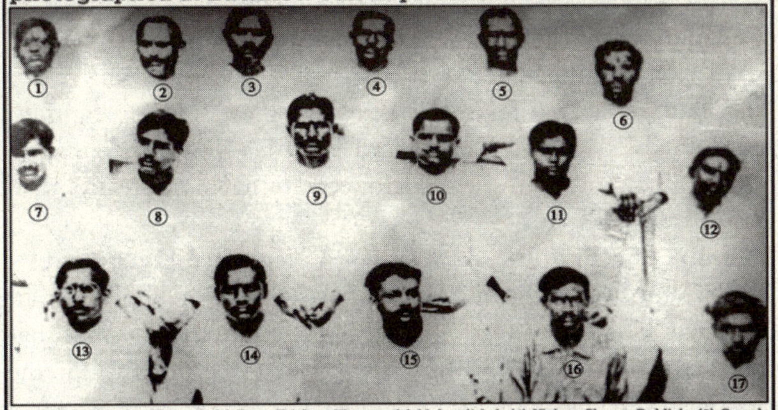

(1) Jogesh Chander Chatterji, (2) Prem Krishan Khanna, (3) Mukandi Lal, (4) Vishnu Sharan Dublish, (5) Suresh Chander Bhattachariya, (6) Ram Krishan Khatri, (7) Manmath Nath Gupat, (8) Raj Kumar Sinha, (9) Roshan Singh, (10) Ram Prasad Bismil, (11) Rajindra Nath Lahiri, (12) Gobind Charankar, (13) Ram Dulare Trivedi, (14) Ram Nath Pandey, (15) Sachinder Nath Sanyal, (16) Bhupinder Nath Sanyal, and (17) Pranvesh Chander Chatterji.

who exactly had fired this shot. Certainly the four freedom fighters who were sentenced to death had not fired this stray shot, although some other members of their group may have done so. In particular it was known that Ram Prasad Bismil had given strict orders against killing innocent people.

Hence, there was a strong legal case for reconsideration of the death sentence and so pleas for this were sent to authorities in India and Britain. However, Ashfaqullah had such a strong sense of the injustices of the colonial system that he opposed this. He initially said that if he had to pray, he would say his prayers only to 'Khuda' and not to anyone else. Later he agreed only when Ram Prasad argued that in order to expose how unjust the system was, all legal possibilities should be explored.

Although they were initially imprisoned separately, fate had ordained that the two great friends would meet once again before death. So the judicial process brought them face to face once again in the death sentence cells (Phansi Kothi) in Lucknow Jail. Here the two great friends met for the last time and shared some of their innermost feelings and thoughts with each other.

Around this time Ram Prasad issued a statement that if at all the highly unjust death sentence was to be given, it should be only for him as he was the leader of the dacoity as well as of the group of revolutionaries, and the death sentence should be taken back in the case of the other three accused.

The legendary friendship of the two great freedom fighters, Ashfaqullah Khan and Ram Prasad Bismil, will always remain a powerful symbol and inspiration for communal harmony in India.

Memoirs of a Ram Prasad Bismil - A Neglected Document

While Ram Prasad Bismil was imprisoned in Gorakhpur Jail, in extremely harsh conditions, he wrote his memoirs. It is said that this text was completed by him just two days before his supreme sacrifice or execution on 19 December 1927.

These memoirs were written on register size pages in pencil. Somehow these were smuggled out of the prison in three instalments and kept in the custody of a local Congress leader named Darshan Prasad Dwivedi. He in turn arranged to send this to Ganesh Shankar Vidyarthi, leading freedom fighter and editor of *Pratap*, based in Kanpur, as it was believed that only Vidyarthi had the courage and the ability to get this published soon. True to the trust reposed in him, Vidyarthi got the memoirs published along with other tributes to the martyrs of the Kakori Case.

Banarasidas Chaturvedi, one of the leading contemporary writers, who was particularly known for his writings on freedom fighters, wrote that only one among hundreds of thousands of persons passes through the circumstances through which Ram Prasad Bismil passed. He added that as a result he considers this to be the finest memoir in Hindi.

Here it may be pointed out that Ram Prasad was also a great poet whose poems and songs were very frequently sung by freedom fighters for a long time. He wrote and translated several important books and set up small publication efforts.

Despite the obvious importance of these memoirs, they have not received the attention deserved by them, at least not in recent times.

A particularly important part of the memoirs relates to the conclusions that Ram Prasad draws from his role as an activist and leader of the revolutionary movement for several years. He notes that the youth have a lot of attraction towards revolvers and other firearms. When they are initially armed and participate in 'action' they are excited and have grand notions of their success in changing the world and bringing a revolution but when the reality of a long and bitter struggle dawns on them, then it becomes a big challenge to sustain their initial ideals and courage. Not many succeed in this.

Instead of this path, he recommends that the youth should work among peasants and workers to resist injustice and achieve justice with a long-term vision of broad-based change. They should prepare themselves for committed educational work (to create a justice and equality based society) over a longer term and only then solid results would be achieved.

In his program of change he gives a lot of importance to achieving equality for Dalits and ending untouchability. Educational work among them is very important, he asserts. He asks—when so many of our own people are being treated as untouchables, how can we achieve freedom in the true sense?

He also gives a lot of importance to improving the status of women. They should neither be humiliated nor regarded as an object of decoration, he asserts. He gives examples of women who played an important role in social change in other countries and pleads for their similar role in India.

In particular Ram Prasad makes a very strong plea to youth to work in villages. He writes that youths who were active in the Non-Cooperation Movement were more seen in high visibility urban areas while the greater need is at the grassroots for long-term committed work in villages. He writes that youths find it difficult and punishing to spend a few days in remote villages.

To ensure long-term commitment in villages, Ram Prasad calls upon youth to take up small-scale, pioneering, entrepreneurial activities in villages to support their livelihood, and at the same time devote much of their time and effort for wider social and political tasks.

In his memoirs, Ram Prasad pleads very strongly for communal harmony and most particularly for Hindu-Muslim unity and harmony. Pointing out to government collusion in promoting communal disturbances, he gives example of how those involved in communal riots were given lower punishments, which were further reduced later, while even those freedom fighters who took special care to avoid indiscriminate or needless violence were given death sentences.

Pointing to his own legendary friendship with fellow-revolutionary Ashfaqullah Khan, Ram Prasad points out in his memoirs that when such a devout Muslim can have such an abiding friendship of complete trust with a devout Hindu (like Ram Prasad), then why can't we have Hindu-Muslim unity in the entire country?

Humanitarian Aspects of the Revolutionary Movement

The revolutionary stream of the freedom movement in India is generally identified in public perception with various violent actions taken up with the larger aim of securing the freedom of the country from colonial rule. However this is a narrow view as this ignores the several organisational and mobilisation activities with which the revolutionary movement was associated, particularly in its later phase.

Another aspect which we should not ignore is that several revolutionaries inspired by the ideal of a more just and equal society, had strong humanitarian tendencies which manifested themselves time and again in the course of their various actions.

Here we share a few examples of this from the autobiography of Ram Prasad Bismil.

Ram Prasad, who was also a great poet and penned many books, has written that the biggest inspiration for him was his mother. She led a very noble and hard-working life. Although married as a child, she later educated herself and started taking a keen interest in social affairs. She often discussed social issues with her son Ram Prasad.

When Ram Prasad started stepping into a wider social life, they discussed this and when he was less inclined to accept her advice, she only said with affection that her only duty was to guide him regarding the likely effects of his action, otherwise he was free to decide what he wanted to do in his life. Time and again she would arrange financial help for him, no matter how difficult it was for her.

However she made him take one vow—that he would never take the life of others not even of enemies. It was very difficult for Ram Prasad to adhere to this vow in the course of all the activities he had to take up as an activist and the leader of a revolutionary party but he always remembered this vow and honoured it to the best extent possible. Taking a life was never the first choice; he always tried to avoid loss of life. When one of his colleagues accidentally fired a shot which led to the loss of a life in the Kakori Case, he was very angry with his colleagues and repeatedly questioned them as to why his strict instructions to avoid any killing had not been fully observed.

Another very interesting aspect of the life of Ram Prasad Bismil was that after he was arrested he had a few opportunities to escape but he did not do so. His first opportunity came due to the carelessness of the police. However the person who had been careless was also known to him as a kind person and the relative of a revolutionary. Ram Prasad deliberately gave up this easy chance to escape as this would have led to the punishment of the kind police official. Another time, a policeman who respected and trusted him gave him an opportunity to escape, but running away would have led to very strong punishment for the policeman. Ram Prasad decided not to escape.

When he was imprisoned (first phase) in Lucknow Jail, he made preparations for a jailbreak and some iron rods were successfully removed. But he could not forget that the jailor, Rao Champalal, had gone out of his way to be kind to him and his colleagues. The jailor sincerely and deeply respected these freedom fighters and as a result of his respect other jail officials were often in the service of Ram Prasad and his comrades instead of punishing and harassing them.

Some of the staff respected Ram Prasad to such an extent that when he performed a *havan* (he was a devout Arya Samaji) they would take the ash of the fire home believing that it would protect them from harm. The guards were so respectful that they ignored the strict rules, and this was partly the reason why the prisoners had succeeded in breaking the rods and keeping this hidden.

When the time for jailbreak came Ram Prasad had second thoughts. For the government he was a very high-value prisoner and if he escaped the elderly jailor, about to earn his pension, would be badly victimized and punished and his family would have suffered greatly. Other officials who had been kind towards them would also suffer. Finally after a lot of thinking Ram Prasad decided to give up his plan of escaping from this particular jail. Later he kept looking for opportunities to escape from other jails but he could not bring himself to betray the trust of those who had been kind and respectful towards him.

During his last days while waiting for his death sentence Ram Prasad wrote that his only regret was that he could not find the time and opportunity to serve at the feet of his mother for a prolonged time. So soft and kind were the feelings of this great freedom fighter who was very unjustly sentenced to death by the colonial government after a farcical trial.

Sarla Behn
Social Reformer and Protector of Himalayan Ecosystem

Bharat Dogra and Madhu Dogra

Sarla Behn was a British lady who made India her home and went to jail while participating in the freedom struggle of India in Uttarakhand. In her last years in India she emerged as a motherly figure for Gandhian social activists in Uttarakhand, an inspirer of the famous Chipko Movement. Leading social and environmental activists of Uttarakhand like Vimla and Sunderlal Bahuguna and Radha Bhatt remember her as their teacher and inspirer.

Born Catherine Mary Heilman on 5 April 1901 in Britain, she was known to be a brilliant student. She excelled in her early work opportunities, but longed for a more fulfilling life. Her quest for a higher aim in life brought her to Vidya Mandir in Udaipur, India. Here, her earlier work for educational reform in tune with Gandhiji's ideas brought her in contact with Mahatma Gandhi and several stalwarts of the freedom movement and its various related constructive activities. In education reform she worked closely with EW Aryanayakam and his wife Asha Devi with whom she formed a lasting relationship.

She was selected to work for hand spinning and hand weaving of wool (woollen khadi) at the Gandhi Ashram in Almora district.

Here she worked in close cooperation with Shantilal Trivedi, a Gandhian activist whose ribs and legs had been broken in a lathi charge while participating in Flag Satyagraha. He always worked beyond his physical capacity. He suffered several physical infirmities yet he always worked with great zest and also a strong sense of humour. Shantilal and Sarla not only succeeded in ensuring good progress of khadi work but also helped to expand the team of devoted freedom movement activists in this region.

As Sarla Behn travelled to remote villages in the Himalayan region with Shantilal, she was happy to see that the Gandhian freedom movement had also spread here and *satyagrahi* freedom fighters could be seen in good numbers in most places.

Around 1941–42 a decision was taken that Sarla Behn would guide a school in Kausani where daughters of freedom fighters could study. This was also the time when the freedom movement was intensifying in a big way with the call of 'Quit India'. Sarla Behn was drawn more and more into the centre of the freedom movement activities in Uttarakhand. She worked in adverse conditions to resist the grave injustice being done to several freedom fighters. The government was going to the extent of auctioning the farms of freedom fighters. Sarla Behn visited families of arrested freedom fighters to arrange help and boost their morale.

Shantilal was arrested. Sarla Behn was first detained at Kausani Ashram and later arrested. Jail life had many hardships, yet those who met her at court appearances were surprised at the peace and tranquillity on her face and in her interactions.

After her release Sarla Behn continued to be active in the freedom movement and in helping families of freedom fighters. Towards the end of 1944 she was arrested again and kept in Almora and then in Lucknow Jail, and then shifted back to Almora. Jawaharlal Nehru spoke in several speeches against the ill-treatment inflicted on Sarla Behn.

On *Raksha Bandhan* (Indian festival) day, Sarla Behn smeared turmeric powder on her handspun threads to prepare *rakhi*s (sacred thread tied by sisters on the wrist of their brothers on Raksha Bandhan day).

When she tied a rakhi on the wrist of the jailor he was overcome with emotions and was unable to turn down her request to be allowed to tie rakhi on the wrist of several freedom-fighter jail inmates.

Sarla Behn was deeply aggrieved by the death of several freedom fighters with whom she had worked due to harsh prison conditions and other adverse factors. After release she continued the work of arranging help and relief for freedom-fighter households who had suffered a lot. Following independence of India she continued her work at the newly formed Lakshmi Ashram where some girls came for a different kind of education and training which prepared them for a life devoted to social service. Several girls trained by Sarla Behn like Vimla Bahuguna and Radha Bhatt later emerged as leading social activists of Uttarakhand.

Chipko Movement. Protecting trees. (Source: Facebook)

For some time she also became very involved in the Bhoodan Movement or Land Gift Movement. This had been initiated by Gandhiji's leading disciple and colleague Vinoba Bhave to bring peaceful change in land relations in the form of land gifts from landowners to landless people (who are generally the poorest people in India's villages). This work also took Sarla Behn to Bihar where she worked in highly adverse conditions for the success of the Bhoodan Movement.

Back in the hills she got closely involved in anti-liquor movements in which her disciples Vimla Bahuguna and Sunderlal Bahuguna were already playing a leading role. These anti-liquor movements had a big impact in removing existing liquor shops from several villages; but what was even more important was the moral impact of this women-led social movement on local men as many of them agreed to give up alcohol consumption once and for all.

Sarla Behn had to leave the hills again to join the efforts for the peaceful surrender and rehabilitation of notorious dacoits in the Chambal region. She was given the responsibility of meeting women family members of dacoits and preparing them for this big change. This was an inspiring experience of peace and reconciliation.

During the seventies the Chipko (hug the trees) Movement had started in Uttarakhand. Gandhian/Sarvodaya activists played the leading role in this. Two leading disciples of Sarla Behn, Vimla and Sunderlal Bahuguna made a particularly important contribution. Sarla Behn emerged as a motherly figure for the younger activists—their friend, philosopher, and guide.

It was encouraging for Sarla Behn to see that some of the girls trained by her at Lakshmi Ashram, Kausani had started playing such an important role in social and ecological movements. Earlier she had sent Vimla for Bhoodan work in Bihar and the feedback she received from Vinobaji's Secretary was that Vimla was like an 'angel from the hills' who assumed very naturally a leadership role in groups of men and women who went to villages for seeking *bhoodan* (gift of land). The activists trained and inspired by Sarla Behn have played an important role in social and educational movements of Uttarakhand which had a wider national and international impact.

Sarla Behn's life and work convinced her of the great need for a complete and basic change in the development paradigm. This change should be in favour of the highly decentralized path based on voluntary frugality or simplicity, non-violence, and spirituality rooted in cooperation for the welfare of all. She expressed shock that the biggest brains prefer to hawk their talent to those who pay the most. She made a strong plea for very basic changes in thinking needed for the post-industrial age. These views are expressed very effectively in her numerous writings. She continued to be a great inspiration till she breathed her last in her beautifully located Himalayan cottage in Dharamgarh (Pithoragarh, Uttarakhand).

Subhadra Kumari Chauhan
Poet and Friend of the Poor

Reshma Bharti

India's freedom movement was a period of high ideals for many writers and poets. It inspired them to devote their literary talents and creativity to the larger cause of liberation of their people and country. In the process these writers and poets accepted many hardships including jail sentences. Subhadra Kumari Chauhan (1904-1948) was one such writer who combined the writer and activist roles with a zeal and devotion that won her the heartfelt affection of millions of people within her short life span of just forty-four years.

Her determination in choosing the difficult path of a freedom fighter is all the more remarkable given the fact that (a) she was a devoted mother of four children, (b) her husband Lakshman Singh, a freedom fighter was frequently imprisoned, (c) there was a time when both Subhadra and Lakshman were imprisoned at the same time with very little social support for their children, (d) Subhadra had to go to jail with a physically challenged baby.

The life of Subhadra is a story of true grit and determination combined with care and endless compassion. Hers is a very inspiring life. She continued to write poetry and short stories of great literary value in the midst of economic hardships, physical ailments, jail sentences, and constant engagements with the problems of the poor and the distressed. Among various public figures in her area, she was invariably the one from whom the poorest had most hope.

This combination of courage and compassion, determination and affection which characterised her life is also very visible in her literary achievements. On the one hand, for perhaps the largest number of her admirers, she is the poet who best captured the life and spirit of the famous Jhansi Ki Rani in her unforgettable poem *Khoob Lari Mardani*. On the other hand, she is also cherished as the composer of some of the most endearing children's poems, drawing often on her interactions with her own children.

Again it is remarkable that her endless problems and public engagements did not come in the way of her very beautiful and close relationship with her children, one of whom, as a three or four-year-old baby boy, insisted on calling her *bitiya rani* (dear daughter)!

Again these aspects of her personality—deep affection and deeper determination—were evident at the time of her jail sentences. Despite very great affection for her children, she did not accept the friendly advice of curtailing her political work (which would invariably lead to a jail sentence) even though her husband was already in jail. So she had to go to jail leaving her three children—led by the eldest daughter Sudha—to their own fate (although helped by some friends).

Secondly, when in jail with her physically challenged baby Mamta, she devoted all her motherly affection to protecting and nurturing her to the extent possible in the grim conditions of the jail. But even in these circumstances, when she heard about the denial of food to 'C' class prisoners, she rushed to somehow provide food to them, regardless of the known fact that this would result in punishment for her, resulting in more difficult conditions for her and so for her daughter as well.

This instinctive urge to stand up for the oppressed and against the oppressor was a very significant part of her personality, leading her constantly to the path less taken, to accepting the most difficult of the various alternatives that existed before her.

But what is very remarkable, in the midst of all this, is that she managed to retain her equally strong instincts for enjoying, and even more for sharing, the small joys of life. Her home was open to neighbourhood children who hung around Subhadra hoping to benefit from her bounty of toffees and lemon drops. When travelling to a town known for its dye work, Subhadra would collect sarees of her neighbours to get these dyed. Her home always remained a hospitable place for local poets and writers (particularly young and upcoming writers) as well as for visiting writers. Regular visitors included Gajanan Muktibodh and Jainendra Kumar, the latter we also see in the unlikely role of arranging free cinema passes for Subhadra whenever he could! A visit to the cinema, a shopping spree to grab some long overdue small comforts for her family during one of those rare times when she had some extra money in her hand; these were some of the small joys she liked to indulge in. More joy came in the company of long-term friends like the famous writer Mahadevi Verma who was also her schoolmate, two years her junior in Allahabad. Both of them used to write poetry as school girls.

Born at Allahabad in 1904 in a high caste (Rajput) family, Subhadra revealed her instinct for both poetry and rebellion at a very young age. She would be angry with her mother for practising discrimination against a low-caste neighbour, and insist on helping domestic workers in their responsibilities. Her elder brother recalled later that she could compose a small poem even on her way to school, sitting in an *ekka*, a horse-cart.

This elder brother Rajju Bhaiya helped in finding a suitable boy for Subhadra, a writer and activist named Lakshman Singh Chauhan who was also his classmate. Lakshman was in touch with social reformers and freedom fighters. This wedding violated prevailing regressive practices of veil and dowry. While Lakshman supported this social reform, some of his family members in his ancestral home at Khandwa did not and they later harassed Subhadra for this.

One of the most senior editors Maakhanlal Chaturvedi invited Lakshman Singh to help with his newspaper *Karmaveer*. The young couple shifted to Jabalpur for this, and this city subsequently became the main workplace of Subhadra, although she also worked in Kanpur, Nagpur, and Bilaspur.

The new place proved conducive for Subhadra to write poetry on issues related to the freedom movement. Her poems on the Jallianwala Bagh massacre were widely circulated. Her most famous long poem was of course the one based on Jhansi Ki Rani and her role in the uprising against colonial rule in 1857. At the same time as an activist she played an important role in taking the various programmes of the Congress to women. Gradually she started travelling to various parts of the province for political work.

The Jhanda (Flag) Satyagraha in 1923 saw Subhadra and Lakshman emerging in frontline leadership roles in Jabalpur and Nagpur. Subhadra went to jail for the first time at the age of eighteen. She was pregnant with her first child, and her health deteriorated rapidly in jail, leading to her early release. Despite her poor health, she continued to participate in the movement. On her return to Jabalpur, her first child Sudha was born.

The shifting of *Karmaveer*'s office brought new economic difficulties. Lakshman took up some work as a lawyer, while Subhadra started writing short stories, which perhaps had better prospects of earning some money compared to poetry. Subhadra's first collection of poetry (*Mukul*) as well as the first short-stories collection won her the prestigious prize for women writers (Seksaria Award) twice. Her stories revealed the constraints, injustices, and dilemmas faced by women in society. Her stories are known for less familiar, less predictable themes and characters. Subhadra's reformist zeal as well as her dedication to the freedom movement is also reflected in some of her short stories.

The life of the young couple was disrupted again by two jail sentences to Lakshman Singh in 1930 and then again in 1932 due to his involvement in the freedom movement. Their sacrifices won them innumerable supporters, but Lakshman and Subhadra also suffered due to the manipulations of narrow-minded Congress leaders who couldn't digest their growing popularity. Despite all obstacles, however Subhadra was elected to the provincial assembly in 1936.

Apart from her work in the freedom movement, Subhadra constantly carried out campaigns for social reforms including the education of women, discarding the veil by them, and abolition of untouchability. In 1941 she was jailed with her baby daughter. She used this time to work for improving the condition of women prisoners and for writing short stories.

With the rising tide of the freedom movement in 1942, first Lakshman Singh was arrested at a very early stage while Subhadra continued to participate in protest meetings. With her arrest also looming large, she prepared their children for facing the tough times ahead with courage. Soon she too was arrested with her small physically challenged baby Mamta who had been under treatment. Here she again struggled for the rights of political prisoners till her health deteriorated to such an extent that the authorities had to release her for life-saving surgery. She survived, thanks mainly to the care provided by her dutiful children led by Sudha.

There was a whiff of romance in these difficult times when Amrit Rai, son of Munshi Premchand asked for Sudha's hand in marriage. But this was an inter-caste marriage and joy also brought some stress. But Subhadra was not one to backtrack on such issues. She boldly faced those who opposed the inter-caste (Kayastha-Rajput) marriage. In fact she went out of her way to invite Amrit Rai to spend a few days with the family before the marriage so that he and Sudha could have a better understanding before starting their married life! Subhadra was so much ahead of her times in her broad social outlook.

1945 was again election time and Subhadra was this time elected unopposed from Jabalpur to the provincial assembly. She plunged into her many responsibilities undeterred by health problems. Although she was associated with Congress, she went out of her way to help sanitation workers who were on a strike with communist support (the Congress was opposed to this strike). While visiting the huts of sanitary workers, she came across a woman who had just given birth to a child but there was no one to help her. Subhadra herself lit the hearth to provide her with hot water. Then she went to her home to arrange other necessary provisions for her.

Freedom came, but also brought the pain of partition. Subhadra and Lakshman made as much effort as possible to fight communalism and prevent violence, but in the prevailing conditions they had only limited success. Before she could recover from this, Gandhiji's assassination came like a thunderbolt for Subhadra. This was a shock from which she never fully recovered. Even in the middle of this great sorrow, however, Subhadra struggled for the right of working class women to pay their last respects to Gandhiji, when they were prevented from doing so due to the high security arrangements.

On 15 February 1948, while returning from Nagpur to Jabalpur after an educational conference, Subhadra died in a road accident near Seoni. This abrupt and untimely end of such an inspiring life of many-sided contributions shocked millions across the country.

Subhadra Kumari Chauhan's enduring contributions to literature, to the freedom movement, social reform, and public works will be cherished for a long time. Her work as a political leader was marked by a very strong spirit of public service with emphasis on helping the poor and resisting injustice, just the qualities which the Congress leadership needed most in the post-independence days. It was a great loss that such a leader was snatched away from the country in the prime of her public life.

Sushila Didi
Pillar of Strength for Revolutionaries

Bharat Dogra

If we look at the activities of the revolutionary freedom fighters during the 1920s and early 1930s, Sushila Didi appears at many places in different roles.

She was born in 1905 in the family of a military medical officer who was inclined towards the freedom movement. Sushila inherited her commitment for the freedom movement from him. Her mother died at a young age and as the eldest child Sushila had to take up a lot of responsibilities for bringing up her younger sisters and brothers.

She wrote a song on Lala Lajpat Rai's martyrdom which was circulated very widely. She first met Bhagat Singh and his comrades in Dehradun where they gave her some pamphlets for distribution in Jalandhar.

Sushila's mother had left some gold ornaments for her marriage. When she heard about the death sentence given to the Kakori Case freedom fighters, she sold these ornaments and donated the money for funding legal services for the Kakori Case revolutionaries.

Sushila took up a job of teaching at a rich man's household in Calcutta, gained their confidence and then used this house as a shelter for some revolutionaries (including Bhagat Singh).

She formed a group of women freedom fighters and surprised Subhas Chandra Bose with their bold presence in the frontline of the freedom movement demonstrations in Calcutta.

When some revolutionaries including Bhagat Singh were imprisoned in Delhi, Sushila also moved to Delhi to help in plans to arrange an escape for Bhagat Singh and the others. But these plans were unsuccessful. In this phase for some time Sushila had to change her identity and lived in disguise as a Sikh man.

As the police were now on the lookout for her in a big way, she had to change her place of stay several times. She kept moving to different places like Calcutta, Lahore, Kanpur, and Allahabad. At the same time when she got an opportunity she participated in the Congress-led freedom movement, giving her identity as Indumati and even served a six-month jail sentence under the identity of Indumati.

Later she married Shyam Mohan, a supporter of the revolutionary movement who had also helped her in avoiding the police.

In her later days she involved herself in Congress-related work and in educational work, establishing a new institution in Ballimaran, Delhi. She left for heavenly abode in 1963. Her immense contributions to the freedom movement will always be a source of great inspiration.

Durga Bhabhi

The Heroine of the Legendary Escape

Bharat Dogra

Durgawati Devi was born in Allahabad. She was known for her courage even in her early days and this quality had ample opportunities for flowering after her marriage to Bhagwati Charan Vohra. Her husband came from a prosperous family but his heart and mind were entirely with the revolutionary youth and their emerging leaders like Bhagat Singh. Durga fully accepted this new role with all its challenges.

They were living in Lahore which was a base for young revolutionaries like Bhagat Singh and Sukhdev. Several revolutionary youths visited their home. Durga was very hospitable towards them and they soon started calling her Durga Bhabhi, a name which stuck to her throughout her life.

An emergency situation soon appeared. The police were looking for Bhagat Singh and he had to escape to Calcutta. So it was arranged that Bhagat Singh would pose as a westernised, high-class Indian while Durga would travel with son Shachi as his wife.

Rajguru, another revolutionary for whom a frantic search was on, would travel as their servant.

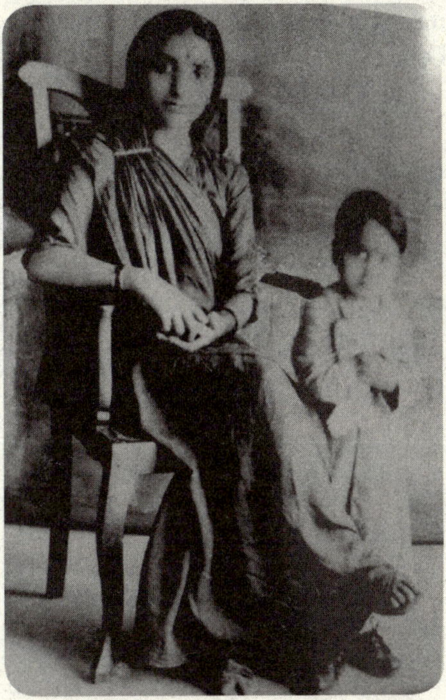

Durga Bhabhi with her son Sachindra Vohra

This escape from Lahore has become legendary and several stories are told about this. Durga Bhabhi played an important role in the successful execution of this escape. She had the additional responsibility of keeping her young son Shachi under control so that he would not unwittingly say anything which could draw suspicion to them.

When Bhagat Singh was imprisoned, plans were made for his jail escape. Durga was again a part of these efforts. Unfortunately due to some accidents these efforts could not succeed.

In one of these accidents, Durga's husband Bhagwati Charan Vohra died. He had been a selfless, dedicated, and courageous revolutionary for several years. Durga's personal distress was deep, but still she continued to take part in revolutionary activities, including a very difficult assignment in Bombay.

By now the police were on the lookout for Durga and it was becoming very difficult for her to hide her identity. Difficulties were increasing day by day. She had to seek shelter here and there, changing her place of hiding, time and again, to avoid being arrested.

She somehow managed to escape to Lucknow where she tried to find a new identity in the mainstream freedom movement, in educational work, and various social initiatives. In her old age she came to Ghaziabad to spend her last days with her son Shachindra, the same Shachi with whom she had escaped from Lahore to Calcutta in 1928.

Many-sided contributions of Durga Bhabhi to the freedom movement are still remembered with pride and inspiration.

Rani Chennamma

Women Martyrs
Backbone of the Freedom Movement

Bharat Dogra Madhu Dogra and Reshma Bharti

Women played a very significant role in the freedom movement of India. Their contribution to the movement was diverse. They were seen in the battlefronts of 1857; they were seen in the frontline of peaceful protests or satyagraha; they were seen in the Rani of Jhansi Regiment of Azad Hind Fauj; they were seen taking up the most courageous assignments in the revolutionary movement; they were seen picketing against liquor shops and they were seen participating most actively in the various constructive programs including the Khadi and Swadeshi Movement. Teenage girls from poor families as well as queens from royal families were seen making the supreme sacrifice for India's freedom.

Rani Chennamma of Kittur Kingdom (Karnataka) fought a very courageous war against colonial attackers in 1824–25. At one stage she even defeated the powerful British force, and then also took special steps for the protection of British women and children. However, when a much bigger British force was sent, then the brave Rani was captured and put in prison where she died.

Rani Lakshmibai

Perhaps the largest number of women freedom fighters became martyrs during the first war of India's independence in 1857–58. They fought bravely on many battlefronts in this war and in many roles. Some of the most celebrated battles are those fought by Rani Lakshmibai in Jhansi of Bundelkhand region (present day Uttar Pradesh). The Rani had raised a special unit of women's army, which included her friends Jhalkari Bai and Moti Bai who were very close to her, to fight the colonial army. They fought very bravely by her side when the British forces attacked Jhansi.

Even after the defeat at Jhansi (in which Jhalkari Bai died) the Rani escaped and continued her brave struggle in Kalpi and Gwalior. She died fighting till the very end against a much superior and bigger force.

Another queen who fought very bravely against the British in the first war of independence was Begum Hazrat Mahal of Awadh. She also constituted a special unit of women fighters and fought very bravely, riding an elephant to supervise the resistance. Later, when her army could not face the superior colonial forces, she had to escape to Nepal where she breathed her last.

Sixteen-year-old Kanaklata Barua led a procession of freedom fighters in Gohpur (Assam) in the Quit India Movement of 1942. When she was trying to unfurl the tricolour flag of the freedom movement she was shot dead by the police.

Matangini Hazra participated in the Civil Disobedience Movement, the Salt Satyagraha, and Quit India Movement, serving prison sentences. In September 1942 while unfurling the tricolour near Tamluk Civil Court she was shot dead by the police.

Sixty-eight-year-old Kumli Nath was walking in a protest demonstration in Darang (Assam) with her son who was carrying the tricolour in his hands. The police fired bullets at her son, but she jumped in front of her son, taking the bullets on her body and achieved martyrdom.

Har Kaur, a domestic worker joined the Jallianwala Bagh protest in Amritsar where she was killed along with many others.

Janki Kumari (Ballia, Uttar Pradesh), Praful Bai and Reeno Bai (Madhya Pradesh), Sindhu Bala Maity (Bengal), Kumari Devi (Shahabad, Bihar), Mathurabai Mate (Pune) also died in police firing and beatings in various satyagraha activities. Similar was the brave story of Mohrani Kurmi (Jaunpur, Uttar Pradesh), Gauri Bai Karia (Narsinghpur, Madhya Pradesh), Srimati Paari (Balasore, Odisha) and Lakshmi Dhere (Wardha, Maharashtra).

Kasturba Gandhi was Gandhiji's very brave companion in several struggles of the freedom movement. Arrested in the course of the Quit India Movement, she died in prison in 1944.

Gurdayal Kaur of Azad Hind Fauj was injured and died in a hospital in Bangkok.

Jyotirmoy Ganguli left a secure government job and died after being injured seriously in a freedom movement procession in Calcutta in 1945.

Pritilata Waddedar died in one of the several courageous and daring exploits of the revolutionaries led by Master Surya Sen in Bengal.

Vanlata Dasgupta participated in revolutionary activities in Bengal at a very young age and died in prison in 1936.

Satyavati was a pillar of socialists within Congress. She was imprisoned several times in the course of the freedom movement and died after being taken to a hospital from jail.

Sarsibala Das was beaten badly in Bardhaman (Bengal) at the time of Quit India protests. She was pregnant at the time and died soon after the cruel beating by the police.

Lakshmi Bai Bhaikar, Subhadra Bai Gosni, Srimati Pujaji, Posni Bai Rajling and Champa Sumade died in the struggles against Razakars.

Sajida Bano and Farichi died in struggles in Kashmir.

Each one of these martyrdoms is a story of great struggle and courage. The brief review above gives only a glimpse of this great saga of fighting and dying for this noble cause by the women of India. It is almost impossible to give a more detailed version of all their stories, so we bring to you the stories of two great women martyrs to give you an idea of the depth and greatness of their sacrifices.

Jhalkari Bai–Brave Companion of Jhansi Ki Rani

Jhalkari Bai was a very courageous freedom fighter who died trying to save the life of Rani Lakshmibai in a grimly fought battle against the colonial rulers in 1858.

Jhalkari Bai

To realise the full worth of her great sacrifice it needs to be remembered that just a few hours before she died, fighting the heavily armed British forces, she had seen her husband, Pooran Kori, dying in the battle to protect the fort of Jhansi from the British attack. Pooran was a very brave warrior and also a very loving husband. They had a very affectionate relationship. They were both young and were bringing up small children.

So it must have been a very great shock for Jhalkari when she saw the death of her husband in this furious battle. In fact for some time they had both fought side by side. Jhalkari's distress knew no bounds when she saw her dearest husband losing his life in enemy fire. Yet, she continued fighting and did not hesitate to sacrifice her own life. Before this, she had handed over their children to the care of close friends.

Unfortunately, such a great sacrifice of Jhalkari Bai did not receive the due attention of scholars for a long time. Some attribute it to the fact that she belonged to a poorer family or the so-called lower caste. In fact, in her personal life also she suffered from the ill-treatment of the rich and dominant persons of the village who conspired against her because they did not like the special affection she had started receiving from Rani Lakshmibai. However Rani Lakshmibai came to her rescue and protected her from this social oppression and injustice.

1857 was the year of a very big and brave uprising against the highly oppressive and exploitative rule of the East India Company in India. Jhansi and Jhansi Ki Rani Lakshmibai played a very important and inspiring role in this revolt of great courage and determination. Lakshmibai had been preparing for the impending confrontations. In this context a very interesting and pioneering initiative that she had taken was to constitute a unit of women warriors who were given adequate training for fighting actual battles.

By this time Jhalkari had won a reputation as a very brave young woman. Legend has it that once when she had gone to the forest for gathering wood she was attacked by a leopard. She fought bravely in self-defence and in the process it was the attacking leopard that perished. Her husband Pooran was recognised as a very brave soldier of the Kingdom of Jhansi. When Jhalkari met the queen with her husband, everyone noticed that the face of the two women had a remarkable resemblance. They became close to each other and so when the recruitment and training of women soldiers started, it was only to be expected that Jhalkari joined this initiative with great enthusiasm. Her husband also helped in her training.

When the attack of the highly armed British forces came, Pooran and Jhalkari were determined to fight till the very end. The Rani of Jhansi had great faith in them, and they were determined to live up to this faith. As a result of their inspiring example, many other people of their Kori community came forward to fight very bravely. For some time Pooran and Jhalkari fought side by side. They, along with several other Kori men and women, made it very difficult for the colonial force to enter the fort. Those women who did not have any weapon or weapon training simply collected stones and a lot of hot water to throw on those who were attacking the fort.

However soon it became clear that it might be difficult to defend the fort. Now it became important to secure a safe escape for the Rani of Jhansi. Hence a safe exit of the queen with a few soldiers was planned. Jhalkari played an important role in this backyard move while Pooran kept fighting bravely in the frontline.

After the Rani left it was important to somehow create an impression that the Rani was still fighting in the fort. This was important for her safety. As Jhalkari bore a strong resemblance to the Rani, she now dressed up as the queen.

Soon after she assumed this role she suffered the great shock of seeing the dead body of her husband Pooran who had sacrificed his life after fighting very bravely in this fierce battle.

Despite this great setback, the conditions were so critical that Jhalkari continued to fight bravely. According to some accounts she also died fighting while according to some other accounts, she was captured and executed. Yet other accounts say that she was imprisoned for a long time but released in her old age.

Whatever the truth of her last days and death, there is absolutely no doubt that Jhalkari Bai will always be remembered as an extremely courageous and inspiring daughter of Bundelkhand and of India.

Pritilata Waddedar – Chose Liberation Struggle over Bright Career

Pritilata is remembered in India's freedom movement as one of the most valiant martyrs.

Pritilata Waddedar

She was born in a village in Chittagong (now in Bangladesh) in 1911. She was a topper in school and was singled out for special merit at her college in Calcutta. She was also emerging as a talented writer.

While her parents were thinking of a bright career, Pritilata was thinking of serving the freedom movement. She always had strong feelings against the colonial rule, but these feelings intensified after meeting Master Surya Sen who was one of the most courageous and respected revolutionaries in the annals of the freedom movement in India. Surya Sen and his colleagues had made big plans for the liberation struggle and Pritilata decided to join them wholeheartedly. In 1932, at the young age of twenty-one, she was in the thick of the revolutionary movement in Chittagong.

Despite her young age and lack of adequate experience, Pritilata gave enough evidence of courage as well as capability in her early actions to win the confidence of her mentor Surya Sen.

As a result of this confidence Pritilata was given greater leadership responsibilities. During one such operation she received a bullet wound. Although she was bleeding profusely, she still succeeded to some extent in escaping. But because of the loss of blood, she could not run beyond a point. It was now imminent that she would soon fall into enemy hands. At this point she consumed the poison she had brought with her to escape capture. Thus ended the life of a very courageous and talented freedom fighter at a very young age.

Her acts of great courage at a tender age will remain a source of inspiration for a very long time.

IN RETROSPECT

Swami Vivekananda and His Message of Hope

Bharat Dogra

Imagine a twenty-seven-year-old *sanyasi* (renunciate) wandering across the vast distances of undivided India, his mind filled with great thoughts of reforming society but with no resources to support his ideas. Imagine also that what he sees fills him increasingly with remorse and anguish as he is revolted by obscurantism, blind faith, rituals, intolerance, poverty, and inequality in society.

But instead of allowing all this to depress him or turn him into a recluse, this sanyasi causes the negativity he sees around him to increase the intensity of his feelings for radical change in society. So that when at the end of his wanderings he emerges to take his message to the world, the intensity of his message is overpowering.

Mahatma Gandhi has written regarding the impact of Swami Vivekananda's work on him, 'I have gone through his works thoroughly, and having gone through them, the love that I had for my country became a thousandfold.'

Rabindranath Tagore called upon people and youth in particular to learn from Vivekananda. He said, 'Study Swami Vivekananda. In him everything is positive and nothing negative.'

Such was the impact Vivekananda had on some of the greatest nation builders of India, and on the political and socio-cultural awakening in the country. But even more important was the message of universal love and tolerance he gave to the entire world. In fact he went much beyond inter-faith intolerance; he wanted people of various faiths to interact in a spirit of enriching each other's faith.

Swami Vivekananda emphasised the need to harmonise the Vedas, the Bible, and the Koran. He said that practical *Advaitism* looks upon and behaves with all humankind as one's own soul. He regretted that this is not yet adequately developed among the Hindus. At the same time, he had no hesitation whatsoever in saying that on the basis of his experiences, followers of Islam had a better grasp of this in practical day-to-day life. Swamiji further said that he was 'firmly persuaded that without the help of practical Islam, theories of *Vedantism*, however fine and wonderful they may be, are entirely valueless to humankind.'

'I see in my mind's eye the future-perfect India rising out of this chaos and strife, glorious and invincible, with Vedanta brain and Islam body.'

'...a junction of the two great systems, Hinduism and Islam—Vedanta brain and Islam body—is the only hope.'

For Swami Vivekananda real spirituality was far away from rituals; instead its true role was to contribute to better life, a more harmonious, peaceful and equality-based life, in a very practical way. He said, 'The dry abstract Advaita should become alive—poetic—in everyday life; out of hopelessly intricate mythology must come concrete moral forms; and out of bewildering yogism must come the most scientific and practical psychology—and all this must be put in a form so that a child may grasp it. That is my life's work.'

Despite his young age, Swami Vivekananda worked at several levels on complex issues. On the one hand he was determined to discover the essence of his religion so that it could be rescued from useless obscurantism and linked to the service of people and all forms of life. Serving God is best fulfilled by serving people and all forms of life was his single message to his co-religionists. His message to fellow *sanyasis* was based on the same perception and he said clearly that the role of a sanyasi should be 'to sacrifice his life for others, to alleviate the misery of millions, to provide the ignorant and depressed masses with the ways and means to stand on their own feet...'

At another level he linked up the revival of his own religion with broader changes for peace, harmony, and tolerance in the entire world. Similarly while addressing youth he emphasised spiritual strength, but also limited it to practical issues like spread of education with special emphasis on the education of girls and women. Moreover education must be linked with character-building and action. As he wrote, 'Education is not the amount of information put into your brain and that runs riot there, undigested, all your life. We must have life-building, man-making, character-making assimilation of ideas.'

'If you've assimilated five good ideas and made those a part of your life and character, you have more education than any man who has memorised a whole library by heart.'

Many of Swamiji's ideas remain remarkably useful and relevant in the present-day context despite all that has changed during the last century. The reason for this enduring relevance is best explained by what Romain Rolland wrote about Swamiji, 'He of all men achieved the highest equilibrium between the diverse forces of thought, and was one of the first to sign a treaty of peace between the two forces eternally warring within us, the forces of reason and of faith.'

Increasing Relevance of Swami Vivekananda's Message

Today it is essential to recall the values of universal love and brotherhood/sisterhood which constitute the essence of Swamiji's message to a world increasingly troubled by fanaticism and revival of religious intolerance in new forms.

Dr Karan Singh says, 'Such is the broadness of Vivekananda's concept of the Hindu faith that had he been around us through some magic, he would have spoken against the idea of "clash of civilisations" as he believed in "confluence of religions".'

In place of the intolerant attitude of religions which placed any one religion in opposition or rivalry to others, Vivekananda emphasised service to other human beings and other forms of life as the basis of all religions. Pranab Mukherjee, the Former President of India has written in a recent review of Swami Vivekananda's work, 'Service to humanity is service to God was the main principle of his gospel to social service.'

Swamiji said, 'After so much tapasya and austerity, I've known that the highest truth is this: He is present in all beings. These are all the manifested forms of Him. There is no other God to seek for. He alone is worshipping God who serves all beings.'

'Humankind ought to be taught that religions are but the varied expressions of THE RELIGION which is Oneness, so that each may choose the path that suits him best.'

'If you go below the surface, you find that Unity between man and man, between races and races, high and low, rich and poor, gods and men, and men and animals. If you go deep enough, all will be seen as only variation of the One, and he who has attained to this conception of Oneness has no more delusion.'

These are the basic values of unity of all human beings and equal concern for all forms of life which form the base of Vivekananda's message to the world. So how is it that religious fanatics and communal elements have been misusing the teachings of Swamiji? This is a question we must ask, because Swamiji's warning against fanaticism is very firm and clear.

This is apparent above all from his famous Chicago speech at the World's Parliament of Religions in 1893.

So it is very disturbing that people tainted with serious allegations of communal violence are using the name of Swami Vivekananda on a large scale. This should be opposed by true followers of Swami Vivekananda as this damages his true legacy.

Another essential and related aspect of Swamiji's message which is increasingly relevant is that he draws a clear relationship between retardation of national development on the one hand and the neglect of weaker sections and women on the other hand.

In a review of Swami Vivekananda's ideas and contributions, Pranab Mukherjee has said, 'Swamiji concluded that the real cause of India's backwardness was the neglect and exploitation of the masses, who produced the wealth of the land...He (Vivekananda) held the neglect of the masses and the subjugation of women to be the two causes of India's downfall.'

Therefore his first message to educated sections, particularly youth, was to serve the poor and the neglected people. He went to the extent of saying, 'So long as the millions live in hunger and ignorance, I hold every man a traitor who, having been educated at their expense, pays not the least heed to them.'

Swamiji was ahead of his times in not only emphasising the education of women but also encouraging them to decide their priorities of social reform. He chastened some overreaching men in strong words, 'Educate women first and leave them to themselves, then they'll tell you what reforms are necessary for them. In matters concerning them, who are you?' Swami Vivekananda rejected the idea of 'writing down smritis and binding them (women) by hard rules.'

Vivekananda had a special relationship with the youth of the country, and hence was closely involved with the issue of educational reforms. He wrote, 'By education I don't mean the present system, but something in the line of positive teaching. Mere book learning won't do. We want education by which character is formed, strength of mind is increased, intellect is expanded, and by which one can stand on one's own feet.'

Swamiji was again amazingly close to modern radical views of educational reforms when he said, 'You cannot teach a child any more than you can grow a plant. The plant develops its own nature. It also teaches itself, but you can help it go forward in its own way.'

Clearly there are many areas where Swami Vivekananda's views are increasingly relevant today. Although some communal elements here very wrongly tried to misuse some of his quotes, out of context, anyone can see that the essence of his message is exactly the opposite of communal thinking. In fact Dr Karan Singh has recently regretted the failure of intellectuals to use Swamiji's ideas to expose the communal elements.

A very important role of Swamiji's messages is to promote inter-faith dialogue and peace efforts at international level.

Relevance of Gandhian Principles in Today's World

Bharat Dogra

Promoting world peace and avoiding wars have always been very important (although seldom realized) objectives for humanity, but in recent decades their importance has increased due to three reasons. Firstly, the availability of weapons of mass destruction (WMDs) means that the destructive potential of war is many times more than ever before. In an all-out war using WMDs, most life-forms on earth will be destroyed in a short time, even though all other life forms and over 95 percent of human beings are not at all responsible for such a war and its weapons. This situation is unique to recent decades, even though life on earth has existed for billions of years and human life in its present form has existed for over 40,000 years at least.

Secondly, a number of very serious inter-related environmental problems, perhaps led by but certainly not confined to climate change, have emerged in recent decades which are quite capable of destroying or seriously disrupting the basic life-nurturing conditions of our planet. In order to resolve these problems before it is too late, we need continuous peace in the next few decades, so that much-needed effort and resources can be devoted for resolving the serious environmental problems without being encumbered or disrupted by wars and related tensions.

Thirdly, wars, weapons, and war-preparations, creating and maintaining related infrastructure are themselves a huge source of environmental ruin including greenhouse gas (GHG) emissions. It is within human capacity to reduce this source of environmental ruin by about 95 percent or so in a short time, also releasing human, material, and financial resources for much-needed protective tasks.

Thus while world peace has always been a very desirable objective, this has been particularly so in recent times. Yet the present day world leadership has not been able to make any significant progress towards ensuring peace in recent times. On the contrary there are all the signs of moving in the reverse direction, including increasing hostility among some of the most powerful countries and the non-renewal of whatever limited agreements that had been reached earlier to reduce the high risks of WMDs.

This failure of world leadership (persons and institutions) at a very critical stage of human and earth history can have catastrophic consequences. On the one hand there is high risk of very destructive wars and on the other hand, even if there is no actual war, war-tensions and war preparations can create a situation in which it is not possible to make continuing efforts with cooperation of all nations to resolve the major environmental issues including climate change before it is too late.

In the middle of this darkness, where is light? Where is hope? One possible source of hope is a great resurgence in the desire for peace among ordinary folk, among common people, among most of us. But how is this possible? One answer is to link world peace to peace in daily life of people. Another and related answer is to link the wider peace objective closely to justice for people at all levels—economic and social justice including gender justice.

In this context the work and ideas of Mahatma Gandhi in particular are very relevant as for nearly five decades he worked for resisting injustice at various levels in peaceful ways, experimenting with various forms of peaceful resistance and evolving them all the time and also taking this message of hope to millions of people. He succeeded in convincing millions of people to embrace peaceful methods for obtaining justice for several decades with continuity, which in itself is a very significant achievement.

This has left a lasting legacy as many struggles in the world including those led by Martin Luther King and Nelson Mandela were inspired by these struggles and experiments of Gandhiji. These struggles in turn inspired others.

Even great revolutionaries who in their own circumstances chose different paths paid a tribute to this messenger of peace. Ho Chi Minh, the great revolutionary leader of Vietnam, declared himself to be a disciple of Mahatma Gandhi. Subhas Chandra Bose, the valiant and great freedom fighter who in certain circumstances had left the path of Mahatma Gandhi, later addressed him as the 'Father of the Nation' and gave him a new title that has persisted for so long amidst many odds.

Despite all this, some limitations of what was achieved also became apparent with the passage of time. India's freedom was accompanied by the most horrific violence related to partition, despite the untiring efforts of Gandhiji and his colleagues to prevent this. This is stated not as a criticism, but in all sincerity to learn from history so that even a more broad-based approach to peace can be explored in future as the challenges ahead of us are truly huge.

The world today needs a peace movement with continuity which links up peace in everyday life with the bigger issues of world peace. When the peace movement helps people in many ways in their daily life, they join the peace movement in larger numbers. All the time the peace movement makes efforts to make people aware of the big issues of world peace, including eliminating WMDs and wars. Hence the support for the big issues of world peace builds up at the grassroots. Governments and international institutions have to respond to this great upsurge in people's yearning for peace. At the same time the peace movement works with selective more responsive persons in governments and international institutions to elicit a better response from them.

In all this we have to learn much from Mahatma Gandhi, just as we have to learn much from his several colleagues as well. This includes well-known colleagues such as Badshah Khan (also known simply as Frontier Gandhi) as well as lesser known followers (like Sri Dev Suman of Uttarakhand) who made great sacrifices on the path of peace. Similarly we need to learn from great teachers like Tolstoy, who inspired Gandhiji, and from Nelson Mandela and Martin Luther King, who were inspired by Gandhiji.

We should also learn from the experiences of the various social and environmental movements (the Chipko and Appiko movements to save forests, the Narmada Bachao Andolan etc.), various peaceful land justice struggles, as well as the even more numerous peaceful anti-liquor struggles with a strong support-base of women, which were inspired at least to some extent from Gandhiji's ideas and efforts. There is increasing relevance of various efforts to check inter-faith violence and to strive for inter-faith harmony, a cause which draws often from the views and commitments of Gandhiji.

Movements for Rights of Political Prisoners

Bharat Dogra

There were several movements for rights of political prisoners in colonial times. Among these, two have a special significance:-

- The fast of Ram Prasad Bismil, Thakur Roshan Singh and the others accused in the Kakori Case in 1925-26.
- The fast of Shaheed Bhagat Singh, Jatindra Nath Das and their other colleagues during 1929.

Both these movements were initiated by jailed political prisoners and supported by a large number of people of India. The second fast attracted nationwide attention.

Another important aspect is that in the case of both these fasts, later death sentences were given to leading participants in these movements and fasts.

In the first case, death sentence was given to Ram Prasad Bismil, Ashfaqullah Khan, Roshan Singh, and Rajendra Lahiri, all of them being accused in the Kakori Case. The farcical trial and the death sentences were widely criticised as being highly unjust. All four were executed (on different dates) in December 1927.

In the case of the second fast, death sentences were given to Bhagat Singh, Rajguru, and Sukhdev. All three were executed on

23 March 1931. Before this, another participant in the fast, Jatindra Nath Das, had died on 13 September 1929 as a result of the adverse health impact of his sixty-three-day fast and the atrocities inflicted on him by prison officials in the course of this fast.

These fasts and movements attracted widespread attention to the rights of political prisoners, their frequent violation, and the tremendous hardships and atrocities suffered by political prisoners who were among the noblest citizens of the country.

Another related issue was that death sentences were being passed on some of the bravest and noblest youths of India who could have been very capable leaders of the country if they had lived. The trials were farcical and highly unjust.

These fasts and movements provided an opportunity to the wider freedom movement to take up the demands of the rights of political prisoners in a wider context and more specifically to demand that there should be no capital punishment for any freedom fighter.

It is a very accepted part of the thinking of non-violence that there should be no capital punishment or death sentence even for proven hardened criminals.

Then surely within the accepted thinking of non-violence there should have been no death sentence for freedom fighters who were among the noblest citizens of the country.

Keeping this in view a Congress-led, Mahatma Gandhi-led movement should have been launched in 1927 to commute the death sentence of the Kakori Case freedom fighters—Ram Prasad Bismil, Ashfaqullah Khan, Roshan Lal, and Rajendra Lahari. The fact that these accused had become symbols of communal harmony and also included great poets among them further strengthened the case for such a demand for commuting death sentence.

The second opportunity for such a movement came in September 1929 when Jatindra Nath Das breathed his last after a sixty-three-day fast. Hundreds of thousands of persons all over the country gathered to pay their tributes to this great martyr. This was perhaps the most opportune time to launch a movement for rights of political prisoners and the first among various demands should have been that there should be no capital punishment for freedom fighters.

The third opportunity for such a movement came in early 1931 when the death sentence for Bhagat Singh, Sukhdev, and Rajguru was announced. The movement for rights of political prisoners led by the demand for no death sentence for freedom fighters should have been launched immediately after this verdict, or perhaps a few months before the likely verdict.

Unfortunately all these three opportunities were missed.

If these non-violent movements whose demands were entirely compatible with the principle of non-violence had taken place, the lives of the noblest youths with the greatest potential could have been saved and the distance between the revolutionary movements and the Congress-led, non-violent movements could have been bridged.

The mainstream movement was certainly the Mahatma Gandhi-led, Congress-led, non-violent mass movement, but if it had received much greater support of revolutionary youths and if there was more continuation in it with the support of youths willing to make great sacrifices, then India would have realised freedom much earlier. The revolutionaries could have also contributed so much more to communal harmony that partition could have been avoided.

Sectarian divides came in more when big upsurges of freedom movement stopped. Continuing work of revolutionaries could've checked communal trends and the wider strength which came from cooperation of two streams could have been used to check communalism and communal forces. If Congress had won the support of revolutionaries with such movements for political prisoners at the right time, then there would have been no reason for Subhas Bose to leave the country in secret for an uncertain future.

When Two Streams Met and Mingled

Bharat Dogra

The various struggles during the freedom movement led by the Congress Party attracted the largest number of people. However the struggles of socialism-oriented revolutionaries led by Shaheed Bhagat Singh also constituted a very important part of the freedom struggle, particularly during the crucial years before the execution of Bhagat Singh.

It is common practice to present the two struggles as separate struggles, the first defined by peaceful means and the latter by violent ones. This however, is not just an oversimplification but also a misrepresentation. The reality is more nuanced, and also more exciting. In real life, the two streams often met and mingled. Supporters and members of the Congress and Naujawan Bharat Sabha (NJBS) often worked in co-operation with each other, or mobilised support for each other. (The NJBS was the youth front of revolutionaries which worked openly, while the Hindustan Socialist Republican Association/Army or HSRA was their secret organisation).

During these years (roughly 1925-31) we frequently find the two sides indulging in fiercely contested debates, but this did not prevent them from co-operation at the ground level. This was helped by the fact that both sides were committed broadly to the overwhelming objectives of freedom, communal harmony, and a broadly left-of-centre view on socio-economic issues. The younger Congress leaders like Jawaharlal Nehru and Subhas Chandra Bose were understandably closer to the revolutionaries compared to elders like Gandhiji.

Both Jawaharlal Nehru and Subhas Bose were invited to chair annual conventions of NJBS during the decade 1925-35. It is on record that Motilal Nehru and Jawaharlal Nehru made donations to Chandra Shekhar Azad, the senior-most leader of HSRA. Nehru visited Bhagat Singh and his comrades in jail and publicly praised their courage and determination. Motilal Nehru overcame the constraints of a serious illness to meet the revolutionaries in the court where their trial was proceeding. He followed these up with legal advice and helped in the campaign for their release.

The Congress was in the forefront of the boycott of the Simon Commission but the credit for a lot of the mobilisation for the boycott in Punjab goes to the NJBS. In the course of the boycott demonstration at Lahore, the most prominent Congress leader of Punjab, Lala Lajpat Rai was beaten brutally by the police and died as a result of this. A Congress leader, Basanti Devi Das, called upon the youth of the nation to respond to this, and this challenge was taken up by the young activists of HSRA.

This was followed by hectic preparations for the Lahore Convention of the Congress which proved historic due to the declaration of the objective of complete freedom from British rule. The NJBS had played a very important role in the successful mobilisation for the Lahore session (at that time Congress was relatively weak in Punjab).

In fact the declaration of the goal of complete freedom was heavily influenced by the growing impact of Bhagat Singh and other revolutionaries on the nation's youth. The Congress realised that if it had to retain its influence among the increasingly radicalised youth, it would have to declare its commitment to complete freedom.

True, this declaration would have come sooner or later, but the radicalising influence of Bhagat Singh and his revolutionary colleagues helped to bring this decision much sooner.

This was exactly the way Bhagat Singh had planned. He realised the important role of the Congress-led struggle but was disappointed by the many conservative tendencies in the struggle which slowed down its progress. Hence the role of the revolutionaries was seen in energising and radicalising the people particularly the youth so that the Congress was pushed towards faster progress on the path of complete freedom from colonial rule.

In addition Bhagat Singh and his colleagues particularly those in Punjab challenged those leaders and forces in Congress which had some sectarian leanings, so that the people became more conscious of the need for communal harmony.

Professor Jagmohan Singh, Secretary of Shaheed Bhagat Singh Research Committee (and a nephew of Bhagat Singh) says, 'It was deliberate and successful planning of the revolutionaries that they will carry out some daring acts which, while causing minimal loss to life, will spread the message of the need for rapid progress towards freedom and socialist ideals. They were very careful about minimising risks to people at the sites of their actions. The actions were followed by rapid dissemination of intended messages for stepping up the freedom movement. In the history of this era, it is very clear how the planning and action of these revolutionaries were highly successful in their intended aim of expanding the freedom movement and increasing its intensity.'

Bhagat Singh and his colleagues were increasingly cautious about avoiding indiscriminate violence. In a statement made in court they declared, 'Revolution is not the cult of the bomb and the pistol. By revolution we mean that the present order of things which is based on manifest injustice must change.'

The fast of sixteen revolutionaries (including Bhagat Singh) in jail continued for sixty-three to ninety-three days and it was in the course of this fast that Jatindra Nath Das died. Hundreds of thousands of people gathered to pay homage to Das. Protests were organised all over India to support the fasting revolutionaries. Congress members played an important role in these gatherings and protests, particularly in Punjab and Bengal, as also in the campaign for the release of revolutionary freedom fighters.

The conduct of the fasting revolutionaries was very much along the lines of other satyagrahis of the freedom movement. It was in the course of this fast that the popularity of the revolutionaries soared to unprecedented heights.

It was becoming increasingly clear to the people from the conduct and statements made by the revolutionary prisoners that far from indulging in any indiscriminate violence, they had planned their activities very carefully keeping in view only the interests of their country and the freedom movement for which they were willing to make any sacrifice and bear any hardship.

This became apparent from the courage and nobility with which they faced the torture and beatings. They endured fasting for very long periods. Even as they saw their own health and the health of their dearest friends collapse before their eyes, they did not surrender. Paralysis gradually spread from one part of the body to another part for freedom fighter Jatindra Nath Das, yet he did not break his fast. Prison authorities used to mix milk in the water, to make the revolutionaries break their fast. Instead of drinking this milk-mixed water, the thirsty prisoners simply broke the pitchers containing this water.

In a paper *Bhagat Singh as Satyagrahi: The Limits to Non-violence in Late Colonial India,* (Modern Asian Studies 43, 3 -2009) Neeti Nair has summarised the impact on the nation:

> 'Soon after news of the hunger strike spread, 30 June (1929) was observed as Bhagat Singh-Dutt Day in a majority of districts in the Punjab. In Lahore, 10,000 people attended a meeting

organised by the City Congress Committee…The Tribune reported that thousands of Lahorians had expressed their solidarity with the hunger-striking prisoners by fasting that day… Bhagat Singh and Dutt were hailed as the honour of Punjab and Bengal…Volunteers from the Congress and the youth leagues marched in procession with red banners carrying photographs of the hunger-striking prisoners bearing the inscription "all for country's honour sixteen young men are starving to death".'

'When the success of these processions unnerved the administration and Section 144 was suddenly imposed, Congress, Ahrar, and Akali leaders including Sardar Mangal Singh and Zafar Ali Khan courted arrest by shouting the newly-banned slogan 'Inquilab Zindabad' along with members of the newly-banned Naujawan Bharat Sabha.'

'Later, when Bhagat Singh, Sukhdev, and Rajguru were sentenced to death, Bhagat Singh Appeal Committees were established in every district of the Punjab. The Tamil Nadu Congress Committee insisted that commuting the death sentence was an essential condition for peace.'

Such a response from a provincial unit of the Congress, that too from distant Tamil Nadu, is a clear indication of the extent to which the relationship between the Congress and the revolutionaries was supportive rather than antagonistic with the latter playing the historically important role of radicalising the former at a time when this was badly needed.

As historian Ravindra Kumar has noted, 'the activities of the revolutionaries complemented the non-violent campaign of the Civil Disobedience Movement and their effect upon popular consciousness was no less decisive than the effect of the Satyagraha Movement.'

Lessons from History for Our Times

Bharat Dogra

A very important aspect of the freedom movement of India was that millions of people, men and women, were involved with deep commitment in peaceful, non-violent actions and movements for resisting the highly unjust and exploitative colonial rule. This involvement continued for nearly three decades. Even school going children were enthused with the spirit of these struggles and created games around these struggles. As they grew up they participated valiantly in these struggles at a very tender age. This ability to raise the human spirit to such a high level for a long time was a very big achievement.

Another important aspect of the same peaceful freedom movement was that the main political struggle against colonialism was accompanied by a wide range of constructive activities aimed at social reform, reducing poverty, and ensuring sustainable livelihoods. Removing the terrible practice of untouchability and promoting social equality in other ways was an important aspect of this social reform. Establishing and promoting inter-faith harmony in various ways was another important aspect of social reform.

Opposing the sale and consumption of liquor and other intoxicants, symbolised by picketing of liquor shops, was important in itself and also because of the support this received from women. Encouraging a more active social role for women was another important aspect and the peaceful freedom movement itself brought forward protesting women on streets in unprecedented ways. Promotion of khadi (hand-spun, hand woven cloth) and making bonfires of imported cloth was symbolic of wider efforts and thinking to resist highly unfair, imposed colonial trade (and the related destruction of livelihoods) and protect sustainable livelihoods while at the same time resisting indiscriminate mechanisation. Promoting public hygiene with voluntary work was an important part of the wider efforts to improve health. There was a concern for evolving low-cost health and education systems more in tune with the real needs of India's poorer people.

In almost all these efforts of the non-violent freedom movement, Mahatma Gandhi played the leading role or an important role. This in itself is a very great achievement that peaceful resistance to colonial rule combined with highly relevant constructive activities maintained continuity for the long duration of nearly three decades. There was even greater continuity in constructive activities than in the activities directly related to freedom from colonial rule.

However, very valiant and important contributions were also made by other streams of the freedom movement which need to be recognized.

For example the great contribution of Shaheed Bhagat Singh and his valiant colleagues can never be forgotten and in fact was recognized by several close colleagues of Gandhiji like Jawaharlal Nehru.

Similarly the great social reform efforts of Babasaheb Ambedkar and his colleagues should get our respect. Sometimes these different streams may appear at odds with each other, but in practice probably what was more important was one aspect of awakening and change adding to and enhancing another aspect of awakening and change. Various sincere people and movements contribute to resolving and reducing a serious problem in their own way; the contribution of all sincere and well-intentioned efforts should be recognized.

What is truly disturbing is that all the deep concern for peace could not stop the tragedy of the great violence of partition. In the last days of colonial rule, the partition of India claimed perhaps one million lives and permanently uprooted several times more people from their ancestral homes and environs. The Great Bengal Famine during the last years of colonial rule took a toll of perhaps four million lives or even more. These facts continue to disturb us deeply and need to be mentioned here because we need to learn from history.

The peaceful struggles for the freedom of India were great and inspiring in themselves, but these did not have a happy ending, as Gandhiji himself stated several times in his last days. This fact needs to be recorded clearly, for the purpose is not just to celebrate the peaceful struggles but to learn from them for future.

Why did the great experiments of peaceful resistance not end in peace? Of course most problems were created by communal organizations and fanatic elements of various faiths, and a lot of problems were caused by the encouragement given to these forces by the colonial government which felt that the freedom movement and free India could be weakened by helping these divisive forces. However at the same time we need to examine why the forces of peace and unity were not strong enough to resist these forces of hatred and violence and deceit. While learned scholars should seek a detailed answer to this question, one brief but important explanation which can be offered here is that the forces of peace and unity were very good but they could not achieve the kind of really broad unity which was needed and several golden opportunities to achieve this unity were lost. There is much to learn from history, particularly the last critical years of the freedom movement, for our difficult times.

Are We Moving Away From the Ideals of our Freedom Fighters?

Bharat Dogra and Jagmohan Singh

The freedom movement of India is a vast saga of great sacrifices, very inspiring courage, and an overwhelming commitment to securing liberty from the bondage of colonial rule; a commitment which enabled a very large number of freedom fighters to endure the greatest hardships for long periods without wavering from their firm commitment. This will always remain a great source of inspiration for persons and groups who want to devote their life to a higher cause. At the same time it is important to remember that while ending colonial rule or moving in this direction was certainly the immediate goal of freedom fighters, most of them certainly looked beyond this and expressed clear and strong views about their commitment to an India based on equality, justice, and dignity for all citizens.

There were of course several streams in our great freedom movement. There were the revolutionaries, best symbolised by Shaheed Bhagat Singh and his colleagues, there were the much larger number of Congress members in the main Gandhian movement, there were the Congress Socialists, the movement led by

Subhas Chandra Bose, and then there were other left groups. There were also various movements of workers and farmers which were very much a part of the larger freedom movement. However what is common to all these movements was that they all were committed to socialism and secularism, while the very sad reality today is that we are farther away from the ideals of socialism and secularism than we were ever before, in the post-freedom days. What is worse—as things stand today—is that we seem to be drifting further away from these two ideals at a relentless pace.

There could be a difference of opinion about the specifics of socialism, but its most essential component is certainly the reduction of inequalities and coming as close to equality of income and opportunities as possible. Many freedom fighters were keenly following events in the contemporary world from this perspective and they enthusiastically supported those changes which showed promise of reducing inequalities and helping the poor and oppressed people. As the colonial rule was based to a large extent on the systemic plunder of our country and its masses including farmers, artisans, and workers, the freedom fighters very naturally wanted a system based on equality which prioritized the removal of poverty and deprivation.

Unfortunately the trend in recent years has been towards increasing inequalities and this trend has further worsened during the last two or three years. Forces have been unleashed which will increase inequalities even more in the near future. In the first three decades after independence there was certainly an agenda of redistribution of land in favour of the landless and poor in rural India but this has been given up now and replaced by a strong role for governments to find land for corporate interests. Crony capitalism and the rapid cornering of resources and contracts by a few favoured top corporate players is increasing and some of these big players have ambitions of near monopolistic control in some key areas. Such factors not only increase economic inequalities but in addition are also a threat to democracy.

Recently the Commitment to Reduce Inequalities Index was released for 152 countries. In this index the rank of India has been placed way below at 132 which means that in terms of commitment to reduce inequality, India is among the worst performing countries. In fact this report has specifically criticized India for this low commitment while also pointing out that there is huge potential for reducing poverty in India by reducing inequalities—just reducing one third of the inequality can result in ending the poverty of 170 million people.

Most of our freedom fighters were deeply committed to the unity of the country based on social equality, respect for all faiths, communal harmony, and non-discrimination. This unity was on the one hand necessary for driving out colonial rulers and on the other hand this was also necessary for justice and peace in post-independence India. With some exceptions India has a reasonably good record of communal harmony and adherence to secularism in the post-independence period taken as a whole. Of course some mistakes needed to be corrected but the overall record was reasonably good. We are not denying that some very unfortunate incidents took place and some very serious mistakes were made, but still taking the entire post-independence period as a whole there was a reasonably good record of secularism and communal harmony in India. But this record has been marred in the last six years because of many tragic incidents of discrimination and violence, worst of all the many incidents of mob lynching which spread panic among vulnerable sections in several parts of the country.

Our freedom fighters for many years faced the cruel repression of imperialist forces and from this as well as from their understanding of imperialist plunder of the country they developed a common understanding of a strong resistance to imperialist forces. The legacy of the freedom movement tells us that we should continue to resist new and emerging forms of imperialism but instead we see big corporate players cornering land and resources in Africa and the government being very generous towards the most exploitative multinational companies including those which want to dominate food, farming, and seeds by spreading genetically modified (GM) crops or in other ways.

When Shaheed Bhagat Singh and his comrades showed the path of opposing imperialism plus bringing in real change by giving the slogan of 'long live the revolution', they were emphasizing the importance of changing the entire system based on inequalities and exploitation, social discrimination, and communalism. Can we reaffirm our commitment to the aims and aspirations of these freedom fighters?

Top Priorities of Five Greatest Freedom Fighters

Bharat Dogra

The freedom movement of India is one of the most inspiring phases of India's long history and produced many leaders of great wisdom and courage. While their list will be invariably a long one, if one has to select five among them who got the respect and admiration of the largest number of people and became a big source of inspiration for them, then there is likely to be wide agreement that the choice will fall on Mahatma Gandhi, Jawaharlal Nehru, Subhas Chandra Bose, Shaheed Bhagat Singh, and Badshah Khan. These five leaders probably got the greatest affection of Indian people during the freedom movement.

While we are all very familiar with the first four, the achievements of Badshah Khan or Khan Abdul Ghaffar Khan were second to none. Here was one disciple of Mahatma Gandhi who in terms of his non-violent resistance perhaps scaled even greater heights than his mentor. It may be said in retrospect that he was one of the greatest, most inspiring, and also the most lovable human beings of South Asia in the twentieth century.

Now we are passing through difficult times when very powerful forces are trying to distort the legacy of the freedom movement in terrible ways. In these times it is very important to remember what the most important commitments of those leaders of the freedom movement who had attracted the largest following were. These five leaders also had some differences, but here we are more interested in knowing what were the most important priorities and commitments on which all five were united.

Jawaharlal Nehru with Badshah Khan

First and foremost, all the five leaders were very clear in terms of their firm commitment to communal harmony. Mahatma Gandhi used to say that this was one cause for which he would be willing to sacrifice his life happily (and he actually did!). Subhas Chandra Bose was very conscious regarding caring about and promoting communal harmony even in the most difficult conditions. Bhagat Singh and Jawaharlal Nehru had a very strong ideological commitment to communal harmony. This is a cause which Jawaharlal never left, neither before nor after the freedom movement, and when some of his colleagues wavered from this commitment he was very saddened by this even though he could not always check this. However, several times, he did go out of his way to challenge and confront those who were spreading communal violence or communal feelings. For Bhagat Singh and his comrades building a society free from communal divide was an integral part of their vision of India and indeed Bhagat Singh specifically said that he had this vision for the entire world. Badshah Khan and his Khudai Khidmatgars came out in the streets in the most difficult conditions time and again to protect Hindus and Sikhs, often in very difficult and provocative conditions.

Mahatma Gandhi with Subhas Chandra Bose and Sardar Vallabhai Patel
(Image from pinterest .com)

Secondly, the other top priority and commitment which all these five inspiring leaders shared in common was to reduce inequalities with a strong sense of socio-economic justice and create a much more equality-based society. If this is a broad and basic understanding of a socialist society then one can assert with confidence that in these broad terms all the five leaders shared a vision of a socialist society. Of course in its details the vision differed for these five leaders but in the more basic terms of commitment to reduce inequalities and create a much more equality-based society all five were on common ground. Bhagat Singh was the most firmly committed to this. Badshah Khan had made a lifetime commitment to building a socialist society by non-violent means and when as a very old man he visited India at the invitation of the then Prime Minister Indira Gandhi one of the main questions he asked Indian leaders was to what extent they had lived up to this ideal. During the freedom movement, Jawaharlal and Subhas were both known for their broadly socialist ideals of reducing inequalities. The commitment of Mahatma Gandhi to reduce inequalities has not been adequately realised and appreciated. In fact some of his ideas had greater potential for reducing inequalities and also keeping them at low levels over a longer time period and that too while following the path of non-violence, but the essence of these ideas was missed in the post-independence days and in fact is hardly appreciated today even by those who pay lip-service to him and his ideas.

It is very important to keep in mind these top priorities of five of the greatest leaders of the freedom movement who also had attracted the largest following. Hence communal harmony and reduction of inequalities constitute the most important legacy of the freedom movement and its most inspiring leaders. This is something that we need to remember in these difficult times when very strong high-level efforts are being made to present a much distorted vision of some aspects of the freedom movement.

Acknowledgement

We would like to thank the editors of various newspapers, journals and news websites who published some parts of these chapters earlier. Special thanks to *Mainstream, The Wire, The Statesman, Janata*, *Vidura*, *The Hoot*, and *Frontier*.

We would like to thank all the media houses, *Creative Commons*, *Wikipedia*, *Facebook*, *Pinterest*, and other open sources for the pictures used in this book.

We would also like to thank our publisher Renu Kaul Verma, editors Papri Sri Raman and Kanagam King, and Team Vitasta for their support.

About the Writers

Professor Jagmohan Singh heads the Shahid Bhagat Singh Research Committee. Apart from teaching at the Punjab Agriculture University he has devoted his life to spreading the vision of Bhagat Singh and his comrades in proper perspective and to co-ordinating democratic rights work.

Reshma Bharti teaches at The Lawrence School, Sanawar. She has written several books and contributed articles to newspapers and journals.

Madhu Dogra has written articles and booklets, and helped to set up community libraries.

Bharat Dogra is a journalist and author who has been associated with several social movements.

Web-site bharatdogra.in

Contact bharatdogra1956.gmail.com

C-27, Raksha Kunj, Paschim Vihar,

New Delhi-110063